TAKING CARE

TAKING CARE

*Monitoring Power Dynamics
and Relational Boundaries
in Pastoral Care and Counseling*

CARRIE DOEHRING

ABINGDON PRESS
Nashville

TAKING CARE

MONITORING POWER DYNAMICS AND RELATIONAL BOUNDARIES
IN PASTORAL CARE AND COUNSELING

Copyright © 1995 by Abingdon Press

This book is printed on recycled, acid-free paper.

Library of Congress Cataloging-in-Publication Data

Doehring, Carrie, 1954-
    Taking care : monitoring power dynamics and relational boundaries in pastoral care and counseling / Carrie Doehring.
    p.   cm.
    Includes bibliographical references and index.
    ISBN 0-687-35934-1 (alk. paper)
    1. Pastoral counseling. 2. Counselor and client. 3. Pastoral theology.
I. Title.
BV4012.2.064 1995
253.5—dc20   95-3958
                                                                                                          CIP

Scripture quotations, unless otherwise indicated, are from the New Revised Standard Version Bible, copyright © 1989, by the Division of Christian Education of the National Council of the Churches of Christ in the United States of America.

Scripture quotations noted KJV are from the King James Version of the Bible.

Scripture quotations noted RSV are from the Revised Standard Version of the Bible, copyright © 1946, 1952, 1971 by the Division of Christian Education of the National Council of the Churches of Christ in the USA. Used by permission.

The poem "Evening Music" on p. 100 is reprinted for *Selected Poems of May Sarton*, edited with an introduction to Serena Sue Hilsinger and Lois Brynes, with the permission of W. W. Norton & Company, Inc. Copyright © 1978 by May Sarton.

95 96 97 98 99 00 01 02 03 04—10 9 8 7 6 5 4 3 2 1

MANUFACTURED IN THE UNITED STATES OF AMERICA

To Mark

CONTENTS

Contents

ACKNOWLEDGMENTS

This book has taken shape during my past three years as the faculty member at Boston University's School of Theology who has taught the introduction to pastoral care course. My awareness of the ways in which power dynamics and relational boundaries can interact was sharpened in the process of teaching this course. I am grateful to the students in these classes. They have explored their formative and transformative experiences in course papers. Together we have become more aware of how our calls to the ministry were rooted in these experiences and how much our present relationships (personal and professional) were shaped by the degree of disengaged, merged, overpowering, empowering, and empathic dynamics of these experiences. Students in the class responded with astuteness and enthusiasm to the earliest formulations of the ideas contained in this book. I am grateful for the learning environment which we created together.

My colleagues Merle Jordan, Carole Bohn, Chris Schlauch, and Sharon Burch at Boston University, Jim Poling at Colgate Rochester Divinity School, and my editor, Ulrike Guthrie, carefully read drafts of this manuscript and gave supportive and insightful feedback. Our conversations helped me nuance and reorganize ideas and express myself more clearly. Most important, they created a sense of companionship that stayed with me during my hours of writing and revising.

The Society for Pastoral Theology has been an enriching and stimulating community during the writing of this book. I presented an outline of this book in a workshop on publishing and had the opportunity to meet editors and hear their responses to my book proposal. It was a privilege to present an earlier formulation of these ideas (Doehring, 1994) at the 1993 Society meeting. It would be difficult to identify all the ways in which my participation at these meetings has shaped my understanding of pastoral care and counseling.

My husband, Mark Jones, and our sons, Jordan and Alex, have helped this book come into being in innumerable ways. Throughout the gestation of this book there were many times in which we experienced the pulls toward disengagement, merger, and power imbalances in our relationships as husband and wife, parents and children. I was continually made aware of how much these undercurrents could sweep us along during crises and transitions. Amid these experiences came moments when we reconnected with a deepened awareness of each other, when we stepped out of power struggles and felt energized by moving through a crisis where everyone felt ultimately recognized and affirmed. The ideas in this book are grounded in these ordinary yet so extraordinary marital and family experiences.

INTRODUCTION

O God,
through the image of a woman
crucified on the cross
I understand at last.
For over half of my life
I have been ashamed
of the scars I bear.
These scars tell an ugly story,
a common story,
about a girl who is the victim
when a man acts out his fantasies.
In the warmth, peace and sunlight
  of your presence
I was able to uncurl the tightly
  clenched fists.
For the first time
I felt your suffering presence with me
in that event.
I have known you as a vulnerable baby,
as a brother, and as a father.
Now I know you as a woman.
You were there with me
as the violated girl
caught in helpless suffering.
The chains of shame and fear
no longer bind my heart and body.
A slow fire of compassion and forgiveness
is kindled.
My tears fall now
for man as well as woman.

....

You were not ashamed of your wounds.
You showed them to Thomas
as marks of your ordeal and death.
I will no longer hide these wounds of mine.
I will bear them gracefully.
They tell a resurrection story.[1]

This prayer took shape during a transformative spiritual retreat when I was twenty-eight years old. I had given birth to my first child eight months earlier and had experienced the goodness of my body and the intensity of a mother's fierce protectiveness of her infant child. When I began a silent retreat for several days, the memories that immediately rose to the surface were of an experience I had when I was twelve years old. I was attacked by a stranger on my way home from school. Now I remembered not only the terror of the assault but its aftermath, and the way my parents were too overwhelmed to be emotionally present with me during interviews with the police. In the months that followed, my mother was unable to speak to me about what had happened. My father tried to "check in" with me several times and I was so overcome by his sense of helplessness that I in turn shut down.

For days, then months, I lived with a terror that it would happen again. The next time I would be kidnapped and no one would be able to rescue me. Gradually these fears faded, but were always somewhere below the surface, ready to rise whenever danger seemed near. It was as if there were two worlds. In one world I was safe and could venture out on my own, putting one foot in front of the other, leaving one place and arriving safely at my destination. The other world, into which it seemed as though I could fall at any moment, was a violent world in which I was helpless.

Somewhat in defiance of these fears, I struck out early on my own, traveling away from home when I was fourteen; living on my own when I was seventeen; and spending a summer overseas when I was eighteen. The fears were most intense when I was midroute, traveling by air from one place to another, or even walking to work or school. Then my alarm system was activated. Since there was no one "keeping track" of when I left home and when I arrived safely (even as a fourteen-year-old traveling on my own by air, I didn't have a routine of calling my parents when I arrived at my destination) there was always a possibility that if something "happened" to me, no one would know.

As the mother of an infant, I returned to these memories with a new perspective. Now I was angry that my childhood trust in the world had been destroyed. I was angry that my reality had been split in two, by the creation of an underworld into which I could be yanked whenever I ventured out into the world. I was angry at my parents and the police. Why had no one been able to really enter my world, and see what it was like for me? Why had my parents and I been unable to communicate in a way that I could express my fears and my needs? Why had I and not they been the one to manage these fears and needs? As a mother, I was appalled that this violent assault and ensuing neglect had happened to a twelve-year-old girl. I realized that if I did not face my memories and the ways in which my experiences had formed me, I would not be able to protect my own child. Either I would numbly let him venture out in the world and cut off my images of violence or I would never let him out the door.

I faced these memories in a setting where I was surrounded by a sense of God's presence. This sense of God's presence was so vivid that when I remembered the assault, the interviews with the police, and my terror at venturing out on my own, I could picture God with me, a silent presence that surrounded me with grace, preserved within me some sense of my own worth, and gave me the courage to take the next step. I could take the next step toward home when my assailant released me. Later, whenever I left home and set out on my own, I was able to take the next step, in spite of my fears. I knew that if I could draw closer to this ever-present life-giving God, I would be able to both love my son as fully as I could, and let him go out into the world when the time was right for him. Writing a prayer was a way of putting into words my faith in this ever-present God. Though the underworld was still a powerful reality, I knew it could not overpower me.

My formative experience of being assaulted and then neglected and my transformative experience of becoming a mother and experiencing God's presence are the existential foundations of this book on power dynamics and relational boundaries in pastoral care. In my *formative* experience I was overpowered by an assailant whose intense needs to have power over another led him to attack a child. He was both *disengaged* from me (if he had been able to imagine what it was like for a twelve-year-old girl, he would never have acted so violently) and *merged* with some fantasy of his own. In the neglect that followed, my parents were overpowered and emotionally disengaged from each other and from me. There was no one within their circle of friends or community to help them make sense of what was happening. No one cared for them so that they could care for me. I remained emotionally disengaged and merged with my images of a violent underworld that could swallow me up whenever I stepped outside. My *transformative* experience of becoming a mother, remembering the assault and neglect, and experiencing God's presence created an empathic relationship between myself and God, myself and my child, myself and my parents. These empathic relationships empowered me to move ahead with grace and courage into a life-giving relationship with my son.

The words I have used to make sense of my formative and transformative experiences—*disengaged, merged, overpowered, empathic and empowered*—describe relational boundaries and power dynamics. When I first began to name relational boundaries as a dynamic of abuse and neglect, I pictured a continuum with empathy in the middle, disengagement at one extreme, and merger[2] at the other extreme. I understood *empathy* to be a quality in a relationship that allowed me to imaginatively step into the experience of another, where there was a constant exchange of information both between me and the other, and within me. This flow of information (both conscious and unconscious) fine-tuned my awareness of what I imagined was going on within the other, within me, and between us. When I was *disengaged,* there was no flow of information. I remained shut down and cut off from what was going on in the other, in myself, and between us. When I was *merged* in a relationship, then I was flooded with too many feelings, images, thoughts, and sensations to really separate out what was going on in myself, in the other, and within the relationship. If I formed any clear images of myself or the other, there were distortions and often exaggerations of what was going on in myself, or the other, or the relationship.

At first it made sense to picture disengagement as opposite to merger. Disengagement was like having thick, rigid intrapsychic and interpersonal boundaries and merger was like having no boundaries at all between me and the other. Empathy seemed to be a midpoint between these opposites because empathy involved having flexible enough boundaries to allow me to step into the experience of another, while at the same time maintaining a sense of myself as separate from the other. The more I used this relational boundaries continuum to understand abuse, the more I realized that disengagement, empathy, and merger did not really fit on a continuum. Disengagement was present when there was merger and vice versa. For example, I could be both disengaged from my true self and merged with some false self. When I was disengaged from the humanity of someone and unable to imagine the world from their perspective, I would create some fantasy about them and remain merged with this fantasy.

The experience of an empathic relationship, involving staying in touch with both the other's humanity and my own humanity, became more possible the less disengaged and merged I was. However, it was not as if there was some decisive moment when disengaged, merged dynamics decreased and an empathic dynamic increased. Rather, there were empathic moments when I could glimpse the depths of the other and myself. In these moments I wasn't disengaged from either the other or myself or merged with some distorted sense of who they were or who I was. These were moments of recognition.[3]

I liken these empathic moments to reading a compass. My experiences of empathic moments, in which there is an awareness of the give and take in relationships and a sense of seeing both the other and oneself in a gaze that honors the worth of each, were a way to get my bearings. These empathic moments were revelations of how I had been or could easily become disengaged and merged. For example, the empathic moment of remembering my assault and neglect in God's presence was like looking at a compass, and seeing the disengaged and merged dynamics going on in the assault and neglect. I could also see the way I had been overpowered, by the assailant in one way and the police in another way. I could see how I had struggled for years, not allowing my fears to overpower me, but hardly feeling empowered when I stepped out in the world. It felt more like going into battle.

When I first started thinking about power dynamics I again pictured a continuum with *empowering* dynamics in the middle, the experience of being *overpowered* (or underpowered) at one extreme, and the experience of *overpowering* another at the other extreme. The more I thought about it, though, the more I realized that one could feel intrapsychically as though one was being overpowered and one could act interpersonally in an overpowering way. For example, I suspect that the man who assaulted me was someone who felt overpowered by what was going on within and around him. He tried to regain some sense of his own power by imagining, then enacting, the assault. Another example of feeling overpowered and acting in an overpowering way was my own determination to take risks by traveling on my own and living away from home. As the time of each leave-taking approached, I would feel overpowered by my fears and needs. At some level I was convinced that this time something would happen to me. The closer I came to my destination, the more I would feel as though I had triumphed and defied my fears. Feeling overpowered accompanied acting in a way to overpower because I was caught in a battle which I would either win or lose.

In an empowering relationship, everyone involved feels energized by a dynamic of give and take, with an alternation between proactive and receptive roles. There isn't a sense that one person has come out on top as the winner. In spite of my continual venturing out on my own, I never felt energized. I felt as though I had won this time, but I might lose the next time. Perhaps, early on or later, if I had been able to communicate my fears and needs to my parents, and they had been able to listen and respond in an empathic way, we could have all felt energized by my stepping out in the world.

Later in life I could experience the ways in which power struggles (within myself and between myself and others) could shift from being overpowering to empowering when empathy was a dynamic of these relationships. For example, with my second son, Alex, I can see how his determination as a three-year-old to say "No," and fight bedtime, bath time, or getting dressed can trigger a battle for control within me and between us. Sometimes in the midst of these experiences I have felt like withdrawing and letting him do what he wants to do because I'm afraid that one of us will be hurt if the "battle" continues.[4] At other times, I have felt pulled into the battle with a determination to win and overpower him at all costs, as though what he needs to learn is that I am in control. When I realize that he is going to battle as a way of finding his voice, I am able to let go of the battle while remaining present as a parent, setting firm limits without overpowering him. Talking afterwards about what has happened is a way of acknowledging the importance of these struggles to define himself. Power struggles can easily become battles between parents and children: "Briefly stated, domination and submission result from a break-down of the necessary tension between self-assertion and mutual recognition that allows self and other to meet as equals" (Benjamin, 1988, 12).

Benjamin goes on to describe assertion and recognition as "the poles of a delicate balance." In order for the process of individuation to occur in children ("the individual's development as a self that is aware of its distinctness from others" [Benjamin, 1988, 12]) this delicate balance between assertion and recognition must be maintained. When a parent's psyche is shaped by childhood experiences of parental domination during critical developmental moments, then parents may slip more easily into battles for control when their children are self-assertive.

I describe my experiences with my son as an illustration of the inevitability of power struggles and indeed the ways in which our most intimate experiences of being partners, parents, sons and daughters pull us into power struggles.[5] Such power struggles, though inevitable and intense, need not be violent and can lead to empathic, empowering moments in relationships. While power struggles are inevitable, a graceful outcome, unfortunately, is not. What we have internalized from our families, communities, and cultures will shape whether our power struggles lead to bloody battles or to graceful reconciliations. The extent of physical, sexual, and emotional abuse in marital and familial relationships attests to how often the battle becomes bloody.

Managing power struggles and the pull toward disengagement and merger in the midst of power struggles is an inevitable part of relationships, not only marital and parental relationships, but pastoral relationships. While interpersonal battles may be more easily avoided in pastoral relationships, there will nonetheless be intrapsychic battles. If such battles pull us toward disengagement and merger, then neglect or abuse may result if we aren't carefully monitoring our thoughts, words, and actions.

This book is about taking care of our selves, those to whom we minister, and indeed all of God's creation, by monitoring power dynamics and relational boundaries in our relationships as a model for pastoral care and counseling. When we monitor the power struggles within us, between us, in our communities and cultures, and the ways in which we are pulled toward disengagement and merger, then we will be able to prevent abuse and neglect. We will also be more likely to experience empowering, empathic moments in our relationships, and use these to "get our bearings."

Taking care by monitoring the interaction of power dynamics and relational boundaries is a theological task. It is one way of seeing our potential for sin and our capacity for violence. When empowering empathic moments come, we glimpse who God is: both the immanent God whose grace shines within our uniqueness and the uniqueness of our relationships, and the transcendent God who goes far beyond who we are. A theology of life-giving images of God and ourselves can be gathered from these glimpses of our relationship with God. Reflecting on the dynamics of disengagement, merger, and power struggles in our relationship with God becomes an intriguing way of assessing our faith, as I will illustrate in the sixth chapter.

Monitoring the ways relational boundaries and power dynamics interact in our relationships means opening our eyes to the potential and reality of abuse and neglect within ourselves and in our relationships. It is not easy to maintain this gaze. Whenever we are exposed to violence within ourselves, in our relationships, among those around us, and in the world, we tend to either shut our eyes or become mesmerized. Shutting our eyes and withdrawing or becoming mesmerized can lead to neglect (as when family members, neighbors, whole communities, and countries refuse to see violence in their midst). Some have argued that our mesmerized, vicarious participation in violence is cathartic and makes us less likely to act violently. Others have argued that it numbs us to violence. Yet others have argued that vicarious participation in violence makes us more likely to act violently.

Whether we avert our gaze or gaze more intensely at violence, we are drawn into the power struggle of violence; we want to identify with the one who has power and we don't want to be like the one who is overpowered. Averting our gaze is a way of "not knowing what is going on" that allows the one with power to continue to have power. In this process we consciously or unconsciously allow the one who is overpowered to bear our experiences of being overpowered that we do not want to remember and re-experience. If, instead of averting our gaze, we become mesmerized, drawing closer to see everything that is going on, we are putting ourselves in the shoes of the one with power. Such power is, at some level or another, awesome to behold.

Our theological task is to neither avert our gaze or become mesmerized by violence, but to name violence as sin and take action to end it. Acknowledging sin and taking action to end violence are acts of faith because the only way we can bear such sights and know what action to take is through our relationship with God.

AN OUTLINE

In this book, I will use case studies from fiction to reflect upon power dynamics and relational boundaries. These case studies for the most part illustrate the violence of overpowering, merged, and disengaged dynamics. I hope that the artistic form of these case studies will make it more possible for us to step within the horizons of the stories, and not feel overpowered, disengaged, or merged, but in the end, empathic and empowered. My experience of reading fiction has made me critical of many of the case studies I read in clinical texts. Often these case studies seem to be written by a disengaged clinician (it's hard to imagine the clinician being able to step into the shoes of the client being portrayed) and with a one-up, one-down power dynamic (the client being clearly the inferior one). When I come across humanely written case studies, where both client and clinician seem empowered by their relationship and there is a sense of reciprocity and mutuality, I feel privileged as a reader to have been invited into this clinical experience.

I have chosen not to write case studies because of my potential for describing my clinical work in a disengaged style in which I am portrayed as superior to my client. Instead I will use fiction to illustrate power dynamics and relational boundaries I have drawn somewhat haphazardly on fiction I have read: *A Month of Sundays* by John Updike, *As For Me and My House* by Sinclair Ross, *Beloved* by Toni Morrison, and *Nuns and Soldiers* by Iris Murdoch. The first three novels are, at moments, almost unbearable to read. These authors neither avert their gaze from violence nor remain mesmerized by it, but describe abuse and neglect in ways that ultimately give us a sense of being able to see and not lose hope.

Following these literary case studies (chapters 1, 2, and 3), I consider how one monitors power dynamics (chapter 4) and relational boundaries (chapter 5) in pastoral care and counseling; how power dynamics and relational boundaries interact to create images of God (chapter 6); and relationships where abuse and neglect are more likely to occur (chapter 7). I also describe how to use literature as case studies (chapter 8). In this chapter I elaborate the ways in which fiction has the potential to widen our horizons.[6] In the concluding chapter (chapter 9), I elaborate a rather pragmatic view of the "mechanics" of contracts in pastoral care and counseling as a way of illustrating how covenants are formed by monitoring relational boundaries and power dynamics.

In concluding this introduction, I want to say something about how *Taking Care: Monitoring Power Dynamics and Relational Boundaries in Pastoral Care and Counseling* is part of current literature in pastoral care and counseling. In recent literature, there is an acknowledgment of the dramatic shifts that have occurred, particularly in religious and theological studies, as we move from a modern to a post-modern culture.[7] The particular ways in which our modern culture has shaped pastoral theology literature are multiple and complex. Don Browning and Chris Schlauch have highlighted the extent to which modern psychological theories and models have dominated the pastoral theology and psychology literature, becoming quasi-religious ethical systems. As well, many pastoral theologians and psychologists have operated out of the individualistic orientation of modern Euro-American culture, with a focus on the healing potential of dyadic relationships. Individualistic, growth-oriented models of pastoral care and counseling resonated deeply with secular models of counseling. Pastoral care givers who aligned themselves with secular models of counseling consciously or unconsciously realized the dissonance between a religious or theological perspective and a secular counseling perspective. In order to not make this dissonance overt, they simply focused on secular counseling models, or kept the two perspectives separate. For example, in verbatim accounts of pastoral encounters, the psychological reflections came first, and then the theological reflections were added as an addendum. The difficulties of bridging these two perspectives were often not acknowledged (as Schlauch, 1993, notes).

Several texts in the late seventies and mid-eighties challenged the Euro-American individualistic orientation of pastoral care that had evolved. Ed Wimberly wrote about the communal orientation of pastoral care in the Black church. He noted that pastoral care in white,

Protestant denominations has been based on the one-to-one model of medical psychiatry. Such a model does not acknowledge economic, political, and social oppression, which, in Black congregations, makes healing difficult. Sustaining people in the midst of oppression has been the primary function of pastoral care in the Black church, and such sustaining has been done through the community. Wimberly's book on pastoral care in the Black church was a forerunner of a new generation of pastoral psychologists and theologians, who are formulating what can be called a post-modern pastoral theology and psychology.

I hope that *Taking Care* will be a contribution to this literature. If this book is used as if it is the only way to understand abuse and neglect in all times and places, then it will simply reflect some of the imperialistic uses of theory in modern times. Within a *modern* frame, monitoring power dynamics and relational boundaries appears to be the key which unlocks the meaning of abuse. Within a *post-modern* frame, the model I propose may produce a relative, momentary meaning that needs to be particular and not universal. As I hope to illustrate throughout this book, attending to relational boundaries and power dynamics is one way of providing pastoral care in a post-modern age, where we are sensitive to the individualism and Euro-American centrism which has so characterized modern Euro-American culture.

CHAPTER ONE

POWER DYNAMICS AND RELATIONAL BOUNDARIES IN CLERGY SEXUAL ABUSE

The novel *A Month of Sundays* is constructed as a daily journal written by a Protestant minister who has been sent for a month to a desert retreat center for clergy sexual abusers. Published in 1975 and described by many reviewers as a hilarious comedy, it is a portrait of a clergy sexual offender that is uncannily accurate. It may be hard for us to think of the protagonist, the Reverend Tom Marshfield, as an abuser, especially when he delights us with his humor, wit, and unabashed transparency.[1] Nonetheless, when readers attend to the ways in which he continually acts upon a sexualized desire for power, they see the extent of his offenses. Besides offering an intricately detailed portrayal of the intrapsychic and interpersonal dynamics of a clergy sexual offender, the novel repeatedly makes reference to the cultural context that supports this behavior. For example, in the midst of his naive innocence about the violence of his actions, the Reverend Tom Marshfield "diagnoses" himself as suffering from "nothing less virulent than the human condition." The adjective *human* actually refers to Euro-American, middle class, and male. Indeed, the Reverend Tom Marshfield does suffer from some of the more virulent consequences of growing up white, male, and middle class in American culture.[2]

We can approach John Updike's novel with a perspective sensitive to (a) power structures that marginalize, and (b) the complex web of conscious and unconscious meanings inherent in both the text and its author. Updike's novel lends itself to such an approach because the protagonist delights in many wordplays, puns, and typographical errors which are used as springboards for streams of associations. These self-disclosures are woven into the journal entries of the Reverend Tom Marshfield like threads of a tapestry showing a pattern. One pattern revealed over and over again is the intertwining of a need to overpower, disengagement from others, and merger with his fantasy world. The outcome of these dynamics is a sexualized need for power over others. For example, Marshfield types that he has been "ompotent" [sic] with a church member. He has indeed been impotent in his attempts at having sex with a church member, a condition he attributes to her unshakable faith. His remedy is to force her to renounce her faith, so that he, not God, can be omnipotent. The wordplay *ompotent* depicts the way his experience of powerlessness and his need to overpower are acted out sexually.

The journal entries portray the extent to which unconscious needs that intertwine sex and power continually drive the character of Tom Marshfield, and, one could say by inference, the character of men who abuse their positions of authority.[3] Marshfield alludes to a parallel between his journaling and the tape recordings made by Nixon in the Oval Office. In the second sentence of Marshfield's journal he notes that he is writing during the "unravelling" of Nixon (Updike, 1975, 3). The sometimes garbled, obscene, and self-centered interjections throughout the texts of both Marshfield and Nixon may be apt portraits of the "human" condition (read: white, male condition of men who abuse positions of authority in the United States).[4] Marshfield's text "unravels" our images of clergymen as benevolent fathers who carry the symbolic power of their positions with grace and integrity.

In *A Month of Sundays,* Updike weaves a complex web of meanings that contains both the conscious, intended meanings of the author and unconscious, unintended meanings.[5] In both author and novel, conscious and unconscious meanings intertwine, with the effect that the unconscious material disrupts and undermines the seemingly integrated, unified whole. This psychodynamic understanding of literary works and their authors counters a humanist ideology of a

> seamlessly unified self . . . a phallic self, constructed on the model of the self-contained, powerful phallus. Gloriously autonomous, it banishes from itself all conflict, contradiction and ambiguity. In this humanist ideology the self is the *sole author* of history and of the literary

text: the humanist creator is potent, phallic, male—God in relation to his world, the author in relation to his text. (Moi, 1985, 8)

Some literary critics have attended to the unconscious dimensions of both the novel and the author by listening for the silences and contradictions of a literary work, much as a psychodynamically-oriented pastoral psychotherapist attends not simply to what is said within an hour, but what is left unsaid: the unspoken subtexts beneath the words we hear. Just as what is unspoken, or what slips out, or what erupts within a client's presentation of him or herself often threatens to "deconstruct" his or her self-presentation, so too the silences, the slips, and the eruptions in this literary text can be used to better understand the plurality of meanings of this text. In its construction as a remarkably transparent journal, the novel appears to lay bare its unconscious dimensions. The protagonist delights in his typographical errors and is zealous in his Freudian interpretations (interestingly enough he is obsessed with the sexual meanings of what he writes and ignores the blatantly aggressive meanings).[6] It may seem as though a psychodynamic reading of the novel would gather its data not from the silences and contradictions of the text, but from all the verbiage of our protagonist.

In my reading of *A Month of Sundays* the silences and contradictions I will listen for have to do with the violence of Marshfield's actions. I will attend to his "not knowing" the violence of his actions. This "not knowing" is combined with his unwitting disclosure of the degree of violence in his behavior. I will also note the paradox of his humorous recounting of his violent antics and wonder how violence can be so funny. I acknowledge that in listening to such silences and contradictions I am not neutral and that my biases may skew my perspective. Someone else, listening for the same dynamics, might nuance his or her reading differently.[7]

When I hear the extent to which the protagonist is unaware of the degree of violence in his actions, I am reminded of the ways in which self-disclosure and transparency do not necessarily lead to healing. The journal entries of Marshfield are as transparent as any card-carrying Freudian analyst could hope for. What remains opaque to Marshfield is how much he is disengaged from others and merged with his fantasies, and the intensity of his need to overpower and his feelings of powerlessness. As long as these dynamics are not taken into account, Marshfield will continue his acting out. The tragedy of the novel is that his transparency leads ultimately not to an epiphany but instead to its opposite, a deliberate (albeit unconscious) distortion of who he is, who others are, and who God is. When he acts upon these distortions, abuse and not healing follows.

In undertaking this reading of *A Month of Sundays,* I will begin by describing the Reverend Tom Marshfield's sexual involvement with the organist of his church, Alicia Crick. Then I will recount his subsequent sexualizing of pastoral counseling relationships with women. I will focus on his abuse of one of these women, Frankie Harlow. After this, I will describe his early childhood as containing the seeds of his disengagement, his distortions (particularly of women) and hunger for power. Finally, I will close the reading with a description of his relationship with Ms. Prynne, the manageress of the retreat center for clergy sexual abusers. I hope that by highlighting these different stories, which in the novel are all woven together, I will describe the way these stories all work together to depict the dynamics (intrapsychic, inter-personal, familial, and cultural) of a clergy sexual offender.

THE REVEREND TOM MARSHFIELD'S SEXUAL INVOLVEMENT WITH THE ORGANIST OF HIS CHURCH, ALICIA CRICK

We begin with Marshfield's description of a fateful conversation with the church organist, Alicia Crick. Interwoven throughout his journal entry are allusions to each other's power or lack of it. She has "ten years up" on him. She goads him; he loves her standing up to him. These allusions to power come at the opening of a conversation about the tempo of a hymn. The conversation shifts from being about hymns to being about her, and Marshfield adopts a pastoral tone, inviting her to tell him what has upset her. She begins to do this haltingly, then lapses into silence. Marshfield breaks the silence, shifting the conversation in another direction. He "boldly" suggests that they talk about *him,* expecting Alicia to say something admiring. She takes the bait, but instead of indulging his narcissism, she gives him a stinging portrait of himself. She describes him as exaggerating himself as a believing unbeliever and in the process teasing the congregation with his sermons. She accuses him of acting out his personal psychodrama on their time. Then she says he is the angriest sane man she has ever met.[8] Marshfield pretends to understand, pretends benevolence, outwardly smiling while inwardly vowing revenge. She declares him to be unhappy because of his marriage, which she describes as terrible. With this pronouncement, writes Marshfield, "Scales fell from my eyes" (Updike, 1975, 32). He describes her as an angel slashing the gray walls of his prison with a blazing sword. He remembers that this conversation took place "early in Lent," that he kissed her on Holy Saturday, that he took her to her home and into bed after Easter.

The conversation that Marshfield reconstructs in his diary shifts in content from being professional, to being pastoral, to being about himself: his anger and unhappiness. While the content of the conversation changes, Marshfield's tone of competition and anger remain the same. The moment of seeming epiphany, when the scales fall from his eyes, is actually a moment of seeing and experiencing her as sexually attractive (as he says, his dear sexy organist). He remains unaware of the need to overpower, which becomes sexualized in his so-called epiphany. Near the end of the journal, Marshfield describes a similar moment, seeing the manageress of his desert retreat center, Ms. Prynne, in a new way. He says he saw through her, with her, and therefore can "presume to claim you as mine" (Updike, 1975, 217). These moments of seeming epiphany could contain an empowering revelation of self, others, and God which opens up new ways of being in relationship. Instead, these are moments when the sexuality of the other is made manifest and with it a compulsion to possess the other sexually.

The ensuing sexual relationship with the organist is described by Marshfield as a return to childhood. Sex is transformed from something serious and businesslike managed by his wife to naked joy and laughter. Marshfield describes them as children, and their bodies as puddles in which they play (Updike, 1975, 35). Extending the metaphor of their sexual relationship as children's play, he says that his body became the Christmas toy that he was entitled to but did not receive as a child.[9]

Near the end of their sexual involvement Alicia becomes angry about the secrecy of their relationship, and Marshfield for a moment is overtaken by a "glum ministerial reality" (Updike, 1975, 82). He remembers then that she is a soul in his care. Seeing her in this way is a rare moment. Marshfield has difficulty seeing her as a soul in his care and as someone with a precarious economic existence. He snidely describes her as handicapped because she is a single mother. He enjoys being in her world and seemingly has no further thoughts about the class differences between them except in terms of his own needs. He notes how different her neighborhood is from his. Her "sparse, raw neighborhood" of tacky houses lacks trees (Updike, 1975, 37). His neighborhood "of imposing McKinley-vintage manses" is "heavily oaked and elmed" (Updike, 1975, 37). He "loves" her neighborhood because he feels assured that Alicia will not abandon him because of her own financial needs (Updike, 1975, 37).

When his interest in her subsides, she becomes angry. She reveals their sexual relationship to Marshfield's wife, Jane. Later in the sequence of events he resolves to fire her. When Marshfield suggests such a course of action to his assistant minister (who also has been sexually involved with Alicia), Ned Bork wonders why Marshfield would "can such a dear little blond bimbo" (Updike, 1975, 144). Marshfield's wife suggests that he is getting rid of her because she became sexually involved with him. She names the imbalance of power, both professional power and economic power, when she tells her husband that he can't fire a single mother who is trying to eke out an existence.

MARSHFIELD'S SUBSEQUENT SEXUALIZING OF MANY OF THE WOMEN WHO CAME TO HIM FOR PASTORAL COUNSELING

Alicia retaliates to being fired by going to Mr. Harlow, a deacon, and disclosing Marshfield's sexual involvement with her and other women in the congregation. For indeed, in the aftermath of his relationship with his organist, many other sexual relationships quickly evolved with women who came to him for pastoral counseling. Marshfield wonders if there is "a smell about me" and if this is drawing women for counseling (Updike, 1975, 132). He speculates that his willingness to "go down" (an allusion to oral sex) is "smelled" by these "troubled women" and that the "traditional sexual ambiguity of the priest" excited them.

These women all seem to have the same problems, according to Marshfield: "That the world men had made no longer fit them" (Updike, 1975, 133). As Marshfield listens to them, he imagines their husbands' common problem as a lack of power in their homes. These "giants" who lead the community and nation become "infant monkeys" at home (Updike, 1975, 133).

How does Marshfield respond pastorally to women experiencing the consequences of these gender inequalities? He notes that within five or six sessions he was "down to sexual details" (Updike, 1975, 134). He adds, "And I did sleep with a few, by way of being helpful" (Updike, 1975, 136). The church building had many quiet "nooks" and crannies for this purpose. Marshfield, seeing these same women listening to his sermons and receiving communion from him, imagines that for them there is a mystical connection between their sexual and spiritual relationships with him. He blesses them for "revealing" a connection where he feels "a horrific gap." He even imagines that his sexual relationships are a form of ministering, marveling at the feelings of "grandeur, an onslaught of *vous* and of dizzying altitude" that he experiences when he places "a communion wafer between the parted lips of the mouth that . . . had received one's throbbingly ejaculated seed" (Updike, 1975, 137).[10] The gap between the experience of receiving communion and fellatio with the same minister within the same church building is indeed horrific and not mystical, as Marshfield would like to imagine it. The grandeur and dizzying altitude he experiences are images of his power over them and not, as he would like to think, images of some mystical union with God. What Marshfield describes as a blessing is in fact a curse for these women: the breaking of a sacred trust and the compounded abuse of their sexual beings and their relationship with God.[11]

Marshfield's desire not only to possess these women sexually but also to break their faith becomes explicit in his relationship with Frankie Harlow, whom Marshfield identifies as the only true believer of all the women with whom he is sexually involved. In sexual encounters with her Marshfield remains impotent (mistyped at one point as "ompotent"). He speculates aloud with her that his problem with impotence is linked with her faith. He asks her to profess her faith. When she does this, a fury gathers in him and he commands her to say she doesn't believe. Then he tries to convince her that belief is

29

ridiculous, describing Christianity as a damn cult and a racket with empty words. While saying this he holds her face up to his level, pulling her skin taut, making her eyes water with pain. Then he hits her and curses her, calling her a "dumb cunt." He yells at her, telling her to denounce her faith so that he can have sex with her (Updike, 1975, 157). Overpowering her in this way gives him a brief erection, of which he quickly tries to take advantage; he then has the gall to both ask for forgiveness and suggest that their attempt at intercourse "was something for you, this time, wasn't it?" (Updike, 1975, 158). Reflecting on this in his journal, he says that if he were to "distill his ministry" he would only find "this single flaw: Frankie Harlow never did get to feel my seed inside of her" (Updike, 1975, 158). And his concluding comment on the incident is that if she had really loved him she would have been willing to "maim" herself. His efforts to "maim" her were thwarted only by lack of time (Updike, 1975, 218).

It is probably no coincidence that Mrs. Harlow (as she is often referred to by Marshfield in his diary) is married to Mr. Harlow, a prominent banker and on the Board of Deacons. When Alicia discloses Marshfield's misconduct, it is Harlow to whom she goes, and he is the one who informs the bishop. Mr. Harlow is described at one point as Frankie Harlow's "living Lord" (Updike, 1975, 175). The typecasting of Harlow as a powerful businessman and his wife as a potential sexual partner is, indeed, how Marshfield experiences the men and women who sit in his congregation, listening to his sermons. The businessmen uniformed in blue suits give "remote approval" to his sermons, while "musk arose thicker than incense from between the legs of their seated wives" (Updike, 1975, 27).

MARSHFIELD'S EARLY CHILDHOOD AND THE SEEDS OF HIS DISENGAGEMENT, MERGER, AND HUNGER FOR POWER

These stereotypes of the men and women in his congregation are evidence of a psychological disengagement that has its roots in his childhood. He writes about the "deadly silence" between his parents. The same silence emanated from their bedroom. He describes them as having few friends and his conception as an afterthought. The lack of apparent intimacy between his parents, between them and their infant son, and between them and their friends seems to create an uninhabited world for Marshfield.[12] As a toddler Marshfield remembers his "fancy" being "engaged" by the furniture. In this silent, seemingly non-interactive household (the only thing Marshfield seems to interact with is the furniture), his strategy as a child was "be good" and "lie low."

The degree of disengagement in the family may be inferred by Marshfield's associations between the furniture and God. He dates his belief in a caring creator back to childhood and his childhood fascination with the intricate details of the furniture and woodwork in his house. The moldings and sashes invoked a sense of God's creative presence. He jokingly comments that the furniture "forced" him to follow his father into the ministry (Updike, 1975, 24).

The theology built upon these images of God seems an empty rhetoric, tied up with his experience of his father's power/powerlessness. What he likes about the theologian Karl Barth is his voice: "wholly masculine, wholly informed, wholly unfrightened" (Updike, 1975, 25). This is the voice he thinks his father ought to have had. Marshfield's neo-orthodoxy is a theological stance that sets him at odds with the liberal humanism of his father and father-in-law. His argument for the transcendence of God, indeed God's discontinuity with creation, seems a model of disengagement: the same disengagement that shapes Marshfield's relationships and becomes the psychological basis for his objectification of women. Marshfield's Barthian stance becomes the way he operationalizes a faith experience of being disengaged from God, himself, and others.

If internal representations of God are formed amid and out of the internal representations of our earliest and most meaningful relationships,[13] then what can be said of these internal representations of God as the maker of furniture? The dire consequences of a faith that seems not to experience God as immanent in people is immediately obvious in his journal entries. Puttying a window sash reawakens his sense of God's immensely caring, discrete presence close at hand (Updike, 1975, 25). In a telling sequence of associations, he says that his next thoughts are about "that redhead . . . her pubic hair as nicely packed around its treasure as excelsior around an ancestral locket" (Updike, 1975, 25). He makes the same associations between furniture, God, women, and sexual desire when he says that when he was a child he watched his father make furniture. This became a religious experience when his father's carpentry helped him understand the furniture's intricate construction. He likens this to the way the women who came to him as "dark bundles and resistant tangles became transparent in being fucked" (Updike, 1975, 191). There is a fusion internally among images of God, women, sexual desire, and power.

MARSHFIELD'S RELATIONSHIP WITH MS. PRYNNE, THE MANAGERESS OF THE RETREAT CENTER FOR CLERGY SEXUAL ABUSERS

Marshfield writes about the intertwining themes of God, women, sexual desire, and power on day 3 and day 25 of his month-long stay at the desert retreat. The task of writing every day in his journal seems to have left unchanged these internal associations. That there has been no real change in the intertwining of his desire for sex and power is dramatically evident in the increasing urgency of his sexual desire for Ms. Prynne, the manageress of this retreat center for clergy sexual abusers. His sexual fuse (and beneath this, his need for power) is set alight when someone writes a comment in his diary one day and he imagines that the comment is from Ms. Prynne.[14]

In his diary entries we experience vividly the psychodynamic roller coaster he is on in his relationship with her. Initially (as he did with the organist, Alicia Crick) he sees her as an ugly, powerful woman. He mockingly likens her face to that of a "large, white, inexplicably self-congratulating turtle" (Updike, 1975, 6) and describes her as snapping rules at him. She holds supreme power in this world he temporarily inhabits and she acquires even greater power when he imagines that she is reading his journal entries. He becomes more and more engaged with her in his imagination. He idealizes her and seductively woos her with lavish erotic descriptions of her body and movements. He declares in writing that he has been in love with her since he arrived. When she interacts kindly with a drunken Native American on a day trip, Marshfield swoons, declaring in his journal that because he has "seen through" her in that moment, he can presume to claim her as his. The degree to which he remains caught in the same conflicts and needs as when he arrived is evident in a journal entry where he describes his problem as a fall "into the abysmal perplexity of the American female" and his cure as another woman, namely Ms. Prynne (Updike, 1975, 201).

He bends the words of his diary with the intent of wooing and drawing Ms. Prynne from her position of power and authority into a sexual relationship with him. He gives five reasons for why he loves her, and then two for why she loves him: because he is here and he needs her. In the desperateness of his need we glimpse the internal fragility he experiences when she is silent and withdrawn. In a panic-stricken moment he feels as if everything is "vaporous" and Ms. Prynne as the only thing that is "solid" (Updike, 1975, 217).[15] If she does not give him a sense of his own body by making love to him, he fears that he will fall through space forever. He writes that he is terrified and feels "up in loose ends" (Updike, 1975, 227).[16]

When there are no further comments written after his long seductive entreaties, he taunts her in his diary, speculating that she may have been appointed to her delicate position as manageress because of her pronounced inseduceability, that she will never "condescend" to him because he is like "a worm . . . the sort you process in batches" (Updike, 1975, 220). When still there are no further written comments and she doesn't knock on his door as he imagines she will, his anger flares and he writes that she is a sashaying cunt, complaining that he didn't sleep all night because he was listening for her arrival at his door.

The last journal entry is broken off, then resumes with a description of Ms. Prynne's arrival and their silent sexual act. The last sentences describe the moment when he sexually enters her and looks at her face. His description of this moment, with its references to "not seeing," "eyes for another," "expressions without a name," and his own face "a stranger" (Updike, 1975, 228) may well bring to a close the diary of a man who only dimly sees others and who remains a stranger to himself, in spite of the hard work of being so unabashedly self-disclosive in his journal. This moment, while seeming to contain a revelation of sorts, offers little hope that much has changed for our hero. By indulging his wishes, Ms. Prynne models the same abuse of power engaged in by her residents. The inequality of their relationship and the intensity of Marshfield's transference toward her should all the more underline his vulnerability. Her indulgence of him ensures that the associations between God, women, sex, and power will remain fused upon his return to family, church and, no doubt, ministry.[17]

When read with an eye focused on power dynamics and relational boundaries, this novel is a potent portrayal of a clergy sexual offender. It is tempting to stay at this somewhat literal level, and create horizons of meaning that arise out of the particularities of this one reading. We need to remind ourselves that *A Month of Sundays* was written not as a moral tale but as a novel with many evocative and ambiguous meanings. We want to honor the plurality and diversity of meanings contained in the text and not bring closure to any reading of the text although, as Moi comments, "All readings are in some sense reductive, in that they impose some kind of closure on the text" (Moi, 1985, 185). We are reminded of how a blindness to the power dynamics implicit in *A Month of Sundays* imposed closure on the text after the initial flurry of reviews and articles, such that the novel has not been considered from a pastoral perspective attentive to the dynamics of sexual misconduct.[18] We need to be mindful of how a perspective highlighting some dynamics of the text may obscure other equally valid textual dynamics.[19]

In commenting further on *A Month of Sundays,* I would like to first discuss the insights of Robert Detweiler, who has described this novel as illustrating the post-modern culture. Then I will use recent writings on clergy sexual misconduct to highlight both the relevance and limitations of this literature in describing Updike's protagonist, the Reverend Tom Marshfield.

THE POST-MODERN CULTURE DEPICTED BY UPDIKE

Doing a psychodynamic reading of *A Month of Sundays* involves focusing on the conflicts and deficits experienced intrapsychically by the protagonist. A cultural reading of the same novel focuses on the extent to which the intrapsychic dynamics mirror cultural dynamics. Detweiler suggests that all the characters in *A Month of Sundays*

> reflect the uncertainty, confusion and cynicism of a culture that has had to abandon the once-fashionable existential pose, with its belief in the freedom to make meaningful decisions, and simply confess that life has become too complicated to be managed. (Detweiler, 1989, 104)

Detweiler draws upon the four sermons written by Marshfield on each Sunday of his stay at the retreat center as evidence of post-modernism.

One recognizes this as post-modern narration: the four sermons display an attitude, beyond a pose of existential alienation, that is mainly confusion; technology is no longer viewed as potentially redemptive but as out of control; language itself is tricky, unmanageable, even demonic; intense self-consciousness frustrates attempts to know and love others. (Detweiler, 1989, 103)

As bleak as the portrayal of this culture may seem, the fact that a coherent portrayal in the form of storytelling is possible is a sign of hope: "an impulse toward reaching an *other* and occasionally even a gesture of community" (Detweiler, 1989, 118). When such storytelling contains within it the giving of sermons, we might react by hearing sermons such as Marshfield's as the ultimate evidence of his (and the culture's) moral and spiritual confusion. Our wish is that the format of the sermon will call forth something better from those ordained to preach God's word. When it doesn't then we can feel pretty hopeless about the state of the culture. Detweiler suggests a different reaction:

The sermon, as model of *in*authenticity in its various guises, still manages to tease us *through* a nostalgia for a naive faith and into imagining what a post-faith faith might be like, can bring us within hearing range of kerygma. Or we could say that the fictional sermon, by so strikingly portraying the absence of kerygma through the medium that once conveyed it, provokes us into imagining its presence. (Detweiler, 1989, 118)

In a chapter entitled "John Updike and the Indictment of Culture-Protestantism," Detweiler (1963) comments that John Updike has much in common with neo-orthodoxy and particularly with Reinhold Niebuhr's criticism of society's "false moralism and . . . belief in human progress that conceals the actual sinful nature of man and society" (Detweiler, 1963, 17). Like Niebuhr, Updike indicts American Protestant culture and highlights the "dual drives of the [Euro-American Protestant male] protagonist toward irresponsibility and independence" (Detweiler, 1963, 14). What Detweiler says of Updike's novel *Rabbit, Run* can be said of *A Month of Sundays:* "The force of Updike's novel, like Niebuhr's theology, is in exposing a society which, because it will not come to terms with its evil, cannot find the redemption of love" (Detweiler, 1963, 24). Updike has:

gone the limit in presenting depravity and perversion as a metaphor of life lived without spiritual orientation. A test may be that the sexuality of [his] characters invites no quickening response but profound aversion. (Detweiler, 1963, 46)

We can focus on the ways in which Marshfield's intrapsychic dynamics are reflective of what has gone wrong in the culture (and especially with those who hold power within a particular culture). In a culture where technology creates disengagement and a sense of powerlessness and where language no longer helps us make sense of our experiences, there is a pervasive "uncertainty, confusion and cynicism" (Detweiler, 1989, 104). Marshfield experiences this helplessness and confusion. When he acts upon this experience, violence follows. Other characters in the novel also reflect these dynamics. The disengagement of both the church community and hierarchy is apparent in that Marshfield is simply withdrawn from the community. There is no process of justice. The retreat center for clergy sexual abusers resembles a day care center with Ms. Prynne as the authoritarian day care provider. The "treatment" of simply writing down one's thoughts in a journal only intensifies Marshfield's intrapsychic experience of disengagement from himself, God, and others; merger with his fantasies; and feelings of helplessness and a need to overpower. There is no more extreme embodiment of an absent, overpowering therapist than Ms. Prynne's reading of Marshfield's journal. The boundary crossing that occurs at the end, with its disengagement and power imbalance, is the final sign of how corrupt this ecclesial institution is. Updike's indictment of the Protestant church in its response to this clergy sexual offender is prophetic and highlights the ways in which clergy sexual abuse is one symptom of our post-modern condition.[20] We can keep this cultural perspective in mind as we review the literature on clergy sexual abuse and reflect further on Tom Marshfield as a clergy sexual offender.

POWER DYNAMICS IN CLERGY SEXUAL MISCONDUCT: NAMING THE SEXUAL AND POWER DYNAMICS: ADULTERY, SEDUCTION, OR SEXUAL MISCONDUCT

When Marshfield diagnoses himself as suffering from "nothing less virulent than the human condition" (Updike, 1975, 4) he mirrors the ethical confusion of his culture in naming his sexual misconduct. The novel's commentators most often name his behavior as adultery.[21] This ethical confusion about the difference between adultery and abuse reflects an unawareness of the power dynamics of clergy-organist, clergy-parishioner, and pastoral counselor-client relationships. An adulterous relationship involves two consenting adults, with one or both of them married. Marie Fortune (1989) notes that there is an imbalance of power in professional relationships which makes mutuality and consent impossible.

While the naming of clergy sexual misconduct as adultery ignores power imbalances, the common fear of clergy that they will be seduced is associated with their feelings of powerlessness. The term *seduction* conjures up images of a powerful woman (or man) bent on enticing a clergy person into a sexual relationship. As Peter Rutter (1992) notes, clients or parishioners who transpose their needs into sexual desire and who act on these feelings with seductive behavior are, by their very actions, revealing their vulnerability, and as such need to have pastoral care givers pay even more careful attention to boundaries and power dynamics. According to Marie Fortune (1989, 121-122) clergy have been preoccupied with wanting protection from seductive parishioners. It is as though they are more aware of the potential for parishioners to harm them, and less unaware of the power they hold and their potential to abuse. A second dynamic that may be an undercurrent in the clergy's fear of seduction is the minister's projection of his wish for a sexual relationship onto a parishioner or client. Marshfield is an example of a minister who hears every word and reads every body movement of women as a sexual invitation, which he aggressively pursues. He even imagines that he can smell the sexual desires of the women seated in his congregation and he describes how every sensation (seeing, hearing, touching, smelling, and tasting) is laden with sexual meanings, which are intertwined, as we noted, with desires to overpower. In the immanence of sex in everything he encounters, Marshfield fits Rediger's (1990) description of clergy with sexual addictions. The trouble with simply naming his rampant sexual acting out as an addiction is that the issues of power are not addressed. Would it be more accurate to call him a power addict, not simply a sex addict? He shows an addictive need to overpower, which is acted out in sexual relationships. Most recent texts of clergy-parishioner and counselor-client sexual relationships name such behavior as professional misconduct. The word *misconduct* implies a legal and ethical standard of professional conduct, where misconduct involves not measuring up to that standard or missing the mark. What is lacking in this term is a description of the impact of sexual misconduct. This meaning is captured in the phrase *sexual abuse by clergy*. Marie Fortune comments that the term *sexual abuse* describes the familial quality of the church, the parental aspect of the role of clergy, and the often parallel dynamics between sexual abuse within families and church families.

Rediger uses the word *malfeasance* to describe "the violation of expectations and the breaking of public trust" and the "distortion of spiritual leadership" (Rediger, 1990, 1). Rutter's (1989) phrase *sex in the forbidden zone* describes sexual betrayals of trust within professional relationships. The term *forbidden zone* describes the irresistible allure of sexual contact that is forbidden and the difficulty of not acting on these sexual feelings.

The novel *A Month of Sundays* and its attendant reviews and commentaries reflect the confusion among many over what to call clergy sexual misconduct, and the similar confusion over what to call treatment. Marshfield names his place of stay a motel and comments that he doesn't want to call it a sanatorium, a halfway house, or a detention center (Updike, 1975, 4), and in the process name his behavior crazy or criminal. Fortune notes that the church's response to clergy sexual misconduct and the way they have dealt with such clergy (often by simply transferring them elsewhere and hoping for the best) have been out of self-interest: "[an institution] tries to protect itself by preventing disclosure of professional misconduct" (Fortune, 1989, xiv).

Fortune (1989, 100) notes that conservative churches have been more apt to name sexual misconduct as adultery. Liberal churches have been more concerned until recently with removing any "policy that prescribed sexual behavior for clergy's private lives" (Fortune, 1989, 101). In the process, they did not consider developing guidelines for dealing with sexual misconduct. Perhaps it is this vacuum in the liberal tradition to which Updike refers when he says:

The primary purpose behind *A Month of Sundays* with its fitful Hawthornian echoes was to show how radically American attitudes have changed in regard to adulterous clergy. . . . As any bishop can tell you, modern clergymen tend to be unapologetic about where their bodies take them. (Updike, quoted in Greiner, 1987, 3)

NAMING THE TRANSGRESSOR: OFFENDER OR WANDERER

Fortune (1989, 47, 156) distinguishes between the clergy sex offender and the wanderer.[22] The offender is "manipulative, coercive, controlling, predatory and sometimes violent" (Fortune, 189, 47). The wanderer is someone who under stress feels inadequate and powerless and who unconsciously seeks out one less powerful than himself (a parishioner, a less-seasoned clergy colleague, or the church organist) and experiences intense sexual feelings for her. It is as though extreme stress can cause a temporary regression that may result in a sexual relationship, particularly when the person to whom he is attracted is vulnerable herself. The paradox of such internal powerlessness is that, in acting to regain control through a sexual relationship with someone unable to give authentic consent, the clergy person is using his external power (the authority of his profession) to enter a sexual relationship in a context where there is no "mutuality, choice, full knowledge and equal power" (Fortune, 1989, 38). In alleviating the internal experience of powerlessness, the pastoral care giver acts out a sexual relationship in which he is overpowering.[23]

The Reverend Tom Marshfield is a chilling portrait of a clergy sexual offender. He aggressively hears everyone as speaking to him sexually. The offender, motivated by feelings of rage, uses overtly violent language and actions in his sexual encounters (as when Marshfield physically assaults Frankie Harlow). With the offender, the victim is made to feel frightened, powerless, and worthless; with the wanderer, the victim is made to feel powerful and special. Given, however, that offenders may use patterns that "range from romantic seduction with the erroneous promise of marriage to forcible rape" (Fortune, 1989, 47), it may be difficult to distinguish a wanderer from an offender, particularly when a pattern with many women over time does not come to light.

The distinction between the sexual offender and the wanderer may often be blurred. Ann-Janine Morey, in a survey of American novels that describe clergy sexual misconduct, brings to light several relational patterns among clergy characters, one of which she describes as "the adolescence of [male] clergy and women who are the necessary accomplices to and victims of his perpetual boyhood" (Morey, 1992b, 81). The youthful, naive, needy qualities of the seemingly adolescent male clergy, paired with a mothering response from particular women, may describe a clergy wanderer. As Morey so aptly says, "This image of the clergy, trapped within the innocence, loneliness, and turbulence of sexually awakening boyhood, is both moving and tragic, for perpetual boyhood demands an indulgent but protective parent somewhere in the wings" (Morey, 1992b, 91).

What is confusing, though, is that anger and the potential for physical violence may lurk below the surface of this perpetual boyhood. This can be seen in the Reverend Marshfield, whose moments of playfulness may evoke an indulgence in the reader such that his brutality is not immediately apparent.

AS FOR ME AND MY HOUSE:
PORTRAIT OF A CLERGY SEXUAL WANDERER

The dynamics of a clergy sexual wanderer can be illustrated through the novel *As for Me and My House* by the Canadian writer Sinclair Ross (1941). The novel is written as the year-long journal of a minister's wife, Mrs. Bentley. She describes in vivid detail what it is like to move into a small, impoverished Saskatchewan town called Horizon, which is struggling to survive years of drought during the depression. The central characters in this novel are the Reverend Philip Bentley and his wife (tellingly, we do not ever hear her first name); Paul, a sensitive school teacher; Judith, a young woman of striking appearance; Mrs. Bird, the doctor's wife; and the church people, a collection of characters made into comic and sometimes tragic figures.

The central events of the novel revolve around two losses in the Bentleys' lives. The first loss is being childless following the death of their newborn son twelve years earlier. The second loss is sacrificing artistic vocations in order to make a living in the ministry. These losses create a bitterness about their lot in life as clergy. This bitterness estranges them from the church and from one another.

When a twelve-year-old Roman Catholic boy is abandoned by his single-parent father, the Bentleys take him in as their son. Philip sees himself in the boy. In particular, he re-experiences his childhood of growing up in a small town as the illegitimate son of a waitress and a student minister. As the church members become more and more antagonistic toward the boy, Philip aligns with him. His own aliena-tion and antagonism toward everyone in Horizon intensifies. At the height of this conflict, two priests arrive from a boarding school and take the boy away with them. Someone in the town has summoned them. The Reverend Bentley feels the loss intensely, becoming cynical and reckless. A week after the boy is taken away, he makes love to Judith, a member of his congregation.

Judith is similar to Philip and the twelve-year-old in that she feels stigmatized by the people of Horizon and trapped within the small prairie town. Judith wishes for something more and works hard to find some way out of the culture and class she is assigned to by birth. Like Philip Bentley, she has tried to gain a foothold in the city, only to return in defeat. Philip Bentley is drawn to her because she is like a more helpless version of him: more externally trapped than he is because of her gender and lack of education. While the Reverend Bentley seems to be endangering himself by recklessly acting out his anger with the town by making love to her, Judith is the one who is most endangered by the relationship. This becomes explicit in her ensuing pregnancy, the condemnation of the townspeople, and her return to her childhood home. That she has no future, as a mother or beyond the farm of her childhood, is made evident in the novel's conclusion. She dies after giving birth to a boy, who is adopted by the Bentleys.

As the novel closes, the Bentleys are leaving Horizon to fulfill a dream of raising a son and beginning a new life in the city where Philip can realize his joy of books by managing a secondhand bookstore and pursue his talents as an artist.

Philip is a sexual wanderer: someone who begins a sexual involve-ment with a parishioner because of intense stress. As can be seen in this novel, Philip's experience of powerlessness, rage, intense loss, and grief are temporarily alleviated when he becomes sexually inti-mate with someone who has even less power than himself.[24] A sense of equilibrium is temporarily regained. *As for Me and My House* por-trays, in rather gothic terms, the damage that one such wanderer can leave behind.

Viewed with a lens focusing on power dynamics and relational boundaries, the novel is replete with images of disengagement, merger, and intense power struggles. These images cluster around themes: nature as overpowering; class differences that cause disengagement; the Bentleys' disengagement from those around them; Philip's disengagement from everyone; Mrs. Bentley's merger with him. These relational and power dynamics are woven together to create a context for abuse.

THE HARSH NATURAL WORLD: MERGED AND OVERPOWERING

In this novel, Sinclair Ross paints a picture of a prairie town caught in the grip of a drought using vivid images of overpowering merger.

> It's an immense night out there, wheeling and windy. The lights on the street and in the houses are helpless against the black wetness, little unilluminating glints that might be painted on it. (Ross, 1941, 5)

> Mile after mile the wind poured by, and we were immersed and lost in it. (Ross, 1941, 38)

Where is God in these scenes of an overpowering natural world in which human beings are submerged and insignificant? In the face of five years of wind, drought, and hail, it's hard to preach a theology that makes any sense. The images that weave throughout the novel are of a blind uncaring universe and lives of grim futility. The Bentleys' friend Paul speculates on how religious beliefs are formed in the experience of being overpowered by droughts and hailstorms. He wonders whether people want to believe in a God more powerful than the storms.

In this novel, Ross echoes a theme throughout Canadian literature, of a people struggling to survive in a harsh land of overwhelming enormity. Their religion, imported from countries whose natures were long civilized and tamed, seems irrelevant and inadequate in a Canadian context. The God of Calvin and Luther seemed to shrink in the experience of struggling to survive and scratch out an existence on this harsh terrain. The country turns them into pagans. The prairie becomes the harsh, devouring mother who blankets everything with snow in the winter and dust in the summer.

When a twelve-year-old son of a farmer dies because his parents, impoverished by the drought, cannot send him for specialized medical care, there are no words of comfort or hope of eternal life. All the father can do is assure his wife that he will sink a fence around the grave to the depth of the coffin to protect it from the gophers and badgers who burrow in the graveyard, which consists of "a fenced-in acre or two of the prairie" (Ross, 1941, 109). Conversations about death are not about God but about temporarily staving off a final merger: the chicken wire fence a fragile boundary between the coffin and the immense prairie with its own vibrant underground life of gophers and groundhogs.

DISENGAGEMENT AND CLASS DIFFERENCES

A second theme is the disengagement and power dynamics created by class differences. Those who are educated feel as though they are different from and superior to those who are uneducated. Paul, who is like a thoughtful version of Philip, comments that "the worst penalty inflicted by education [is] the way it separates you from the people who are really closest to you, among whom you would otherwise belong" (Ross, 1941, 20). The Bentleys do have the opportunity of joining a small intellectual community in Horizon, made up of Paul, who is a school teacher, the doctor and his wife, and Judith, but they each hold themselves aloof from people who are perceptive and sensitive to their needs and pain. Mrs. Bentley keeps her emotional distance from Paul, Judith, and Mrs. Bird when they see her pain and want to draw close to her. She explains her disengagement by saying that she never gets along with women very well.

Their stance of aloofness from church people and their peers and the roles they assume as clergy keep them disconnected, not only from those around them but from themselves. Mrs. Bentley is proud of her detachment (Ross, 1941, 16) and notes that the false fronted towns they've lived in have taught her "to erect a false front of my own, live my own life, keep myself intact" (Ross, 1941, 9). She goes on to describe the intense inferiority she can feel when she wears a shabby old hat and coat to play the organ. Her words highlight how the false front of intellectual superiority and disengagement is a way of compensating for feelings of inferiority, particularly as a woman.

When their context temporarily shifts from being clergy in a small town to being a couple on vacation at a friend's family ranch for a few weeks, Mrs. Bentley realizes how much she and her husband have internalized the role of being minister and minister's wife. She hears how her husband's attempts to make conversation make him sound "like a priggish young evangelist" (Ross, 1941, 93). She catches in her own conversations "a hint of the benediction" (Ross, 1941, 93). The lack of intimacy with one another or with peers becomes evident on this vacation when they leave behind the false fronted town of Horizon and find themselves with their own false fronts.

PHILIP'S DISENGAGEMENT

We can understand Philip's sexual involvement with Judith as a consequence of destructive power dynamics and disengagement. Mrs. Bentley describes her husband as an isolated man. The effects of this isolation are most telling in terms of his art, which has shifted from having "feeling and humanity in it . . . warm and positive and forthright" to being "distorted, intensified, alive with thin cold, bitter life" (Ross, 1941, 17).

Hand in hand with these descriptions of isolation are Mrs. Bentley's descriptions of the power struggles that go on between them. She describes the dance that has evolved between them. Whenever "he gives himself" to her—words that she uses to describe the experience of coming close to one another—(Ross, 1941, 23) what follows is always "a sudden mustering of self sufficiency, a repudiating swing the other way." She understands this as his resentment of his need of her, which "somehow . . . makes him feel weak, a little unmanly" (Ross, 1941, 23). Being close is associated with merger (giving himself) and a loss of manly power. Survival depends on re-establishing power and boundaries (self-sufficiency). Mrs. Bentley comments that when Philip smoked they were pulled together as "partners in conspiracy" (Ross, 1941, 14). While it seems an image of intimacy, in fact the ritual of pipe lighting and smoking, with its sense of conspiracy against a disapproving congregation, is within the context of a power struggle with "the Main Streets of the World."

MRS. BENTLEY'S MERGER

Mr. Bentley's stance of disengagement is opposite to Mrs. Bentley's sense of merger with her husband. She seemingly can read him like an open book, and even feel beneath his skin and behind a closed door, to what is going on inside of him. When he sits all afternoon in his study with the door shut, she constantly pictures him with "his lips set, his eyes dry and hurt" (Ross, 1941, 15). She is sensitive to his every mood, merged as she is with him, and seems to know immediately when he begins a sexual relationship with Judith. He, in contrast, seems to be oblivious to what goes on within her.

Mrs. Bentley knows that when she gave up her art (music) she became merged with her husband. She describes how she forgot her own dreams of studying music and instead read his books, so that she could "reach up to his intellect, be a good companion, . . . nod comprehendingly . . . Submitting to him that way, yielding my identity—it seemed what life was intended for" (Ross, 1941, 16). This leaves her with a merged world, a constant straining after a man who keeps his distance. She yearns to have him notice her and when he does, she feels as though his attention "arranges my world for me, strengthens and quickens it, makes it immune to all other worlds" (Ross, 1941, 16).

On the one hand, she describes how she has been trying to possess her husband and "absorb his life in mine" (Ross, 1941, 64). On the other hand, she realizes how, in attempting to gain psychological control of him, she has lost herself, and is, in fact, even more disempowered than her husband:

> I've whittled myself hollow that I might enclose him and hold him, and when he shakes me off I'm just a shell. (Ross, 1941, 75)

Despairingly, she describes herself as rootless, a fungus or parasite who will die if it is thrown off (Ross, 1941, 151).

As the novel ends, they are standing on the edge of what seems to be a new world: they are parents, they are leaving behind ministry and their false-fronted town, Philip is following a truer vocation. How much this will be a new world depends, however, on the extent to which they can move from disengaged, merged dynamics where power balances are awry to more empathic, empowered relationships.

The novel, in its last words, does not sound a note of hope. Philip is questioning his wife on her choice of the name Philip for their adopted son. He wonders whether with two Philips in the house, she won't get mixed up, not knowing which of them is which. In her mind, she answers that he is right, and that she wants it so. These last words in the novel underline that the dynamics of merger continue.

We as readers are reminded that this seemingly new life is founded on the death of Judith, the most explicit casualty of these power dynamics and relational boundaries gone awry. Without a radical repentance, wherein eyes are opened to the extent of destruction caused by merged, disengaged, and overpowering dynamics, there will be no new life and no end of destruction.

CHAPTER TWO

THE OVER-POWERING DISENGAGEMENT OF RACISM

Reflecting upon a novel by an African American is an opportunity to see what difference race makes when it comes to power dynamics and relational boundaries. In this chapter, I will discuss Toni Morrison's novel *Beloved,* attending to power dynamics and relational boundaries. This novel vividly describes the dehumanization of African American men, women, and children that occurred during slavery and throughout the period of Reconstruction.

In concluding this chapter, I will consider some of the themes from Morrison's novel—the violence of racial stereotypes, the sustaining role of the neighborhood, the consequences of rugged individualism, and the need for a faith that can sustain one in the midst of violence—in the light of the pastoral theological writings of Ed Wimberly, Archie Smith, and James Evans. They suggest that African American Christianity is a viable response not only to racial violence but the post-modern condition.

TONI MORRISON'S *BELOVED*

Simply speaking, this novel is a ghost story. The ghost is the not yet two-year-old girl killed by her mother, Sethe. The slaying happens when Sethe's slave owner, Schoolteacher, arrives to recapture her and her children. Sethe, hiding in the woodshed, begins to kill each of her children. She is fiercely determined that they will not go back into the hell of slavery. She is stopped after the first murder. Her desperate strategy works in that the slave owner, horrified, backs away and flees from her. Sethe is arrested and when she returns home from jail remains isolated. She is ostracized by her community, not for the murder in particular, but for her "pride" and self-sufficiency. Her house becomes haunted by the angry, anguished spirit of her slain child. When the ghost departs, a strange woman arrives at Sethe's door and moves in with her. This woman is precisely the age of Sethe's murdered child, had she lived. This woman appears to have no origins and bears the name written on the child's tombstone, Beloved. She slowly takes over the household. Finally, Sethe's neighbors, activated by the old man who first helped Sethe to freedom, gather to exorcise Beloved from the house.

In this novel there is some movement from disengagement to empathy[1] and from being overpowered to being empowered. This movement occurs intrapsychically in the main characters of Sethe and her lover, Paul; and communally among the freed black men and women of Sethe's neighborhood in Cincinnati, who move from a disengaged stance to an empathic stance in relation to Sethe. At a cultural level, there is no movement among most of the white folk, who remain in an overpowering stance that is both disengaged from the humanity of the African American people and caught in a frenzied hatred, merged with what these people represent to them.[2] Throughout the story these white folk become, if anything, more violent as the country moves through the transition of the end of legalized slavery.

One way to view the way relational boundaries and power dynamics interact in this novel is to focus first on the largest social system of a white racist society leading up to and through the Civil War and into the period of Reconstruction. Next we can focus on the neighborhood of blacks who have escaped slavery to live in Cincinnati. Then we can look at the intrapsychic dynamics of the novel's characters: those who live within the haunted house at 124 Bluestone Road.

THE OVERPOWERING EURO-AMERICANS

More than anything else, Morrison's novel *Beloved* portrays the brutality of this racist society: how men and women are branded and treated as animals; how children are torn from their mothers in their earliest weeks of life; how husbands must watch as their wives are raped and beaten; how children must watch as their parents are knocked down or hanged. Through attention to the minute details of this violence, Morrison weaves a tapestry of suffering that is almost unbearable to view. Reading is made bearable by the lyricism of Morrison's style, which details the violence of racism in a way that illuminates the humanity of each character. Morrison does not simply recount the violence of slavery[3] in a chronological retelling. Instead, she tells the story piecemeal, moving backward and forward in time, depicting the way Sethe remembers: specifically the way Sethe alternates between freezing and being flooded by painful memories. Morrison draws the reader into Sethe's inner world, and the reader is actively involved in making sense of the bits and pieces of the story Morrison retells.

Morrison pays particular attention to the relationships between mothers and their children. She invites us to stand in the place of Sethe when as a toddler she was separated from her mother three weeks after birth and only knew her mother by the brand mark burned on her mother's skin.[4] Morrison at moments uses disjointed language and word repetition to draw the reader into the inner world of a young child trying to make sense of her experience with only the beginnings of language and without the interchange of language between mother and child. What comes through in this urgent repetitive chanting of disjointed words is a child's yearning for physical contact, for nestling in a mother's lap. The anguish of mothers and their children wails throughout the pages of this book.[5]

The extent to which the Euro-Americans are disengaged from the humanity of these African American men, women, and children is staggering. Instead of being engaged with the humanity of the African Americans, the Euro-American characters remain profoundly merged with their projections of who these African Americans are, and act upon these projections with hatred and violence. This disengagement from the humanity of another and merger with projections of the other were enacted in the stereotypes of slaves. One such stereotype is the small cast-iron figure of a kneeling black boy which sits on a shelf next to the kitchen door of a Euro-American household. With its head pulled back, its mouth gapes open like a cup, full of coins. At the base of the figure are the words, "At Yo Service" (Morrison, 1987, 255). An equally chilling stereotype is the notion that African Americans are part animal.

Schoolteacher, a slave owner in *Beloved,* measures his slaves and keeps records like some amateur naturalist. He concocts the "experiment" of having his nephew suck Sethe's breast as though she is an animal. These stereotypes of subservience and of bestiality are consequences of the extreme disengagement from the humanity of African Americans and the need to have power over whatever distortions they project upon these people.

One consequence of the Euro-American's disengagement from the humanity of African Americans and their merger with distorted images of African Americans is that some of the African American characters in the novel feel as though they are not endowed with human selves. These characters have internalized a sense of soul-less-ness. At the end of her life, Baby Suggs, Sethe's mother-in-law, describes her experience of being a person without a self. She describes her inner being as a "desolated center where the self that was no self made its home" (Morrison, 1987, 140). She realizes that she knows more about each of her children who disappeared or were snatched away from her than she knows about herself. She cannot answer the most basic questions about childhood: whether she was pretty or could sing and whether or not her mother would like her if she had known her. These questions are like mirrors which Baby Suggs holds up to herself, aware that she sees no reflection. She cannot see her self because she has lived in a society that not only was blind to her self, but smashed any glimmerings of self that she had.

Baby Suggs' experience of soul-less-ness is especially poignant when one considers the charismatic ministry she had throughout much of her life as a freed slave. Her presence had such charisma that she invoked an electrifying sense of God's presence in those around her. Perhaps her immersion in God's spirit made her more acutely aware of the soul-depriving hatred around her. It was as though she lived in two worlds: the spiritual world where she felt a profound connection and the racist world where there was profound disconnection and distortion of her very soul. In the end she gave up her charismatic ministry in her neighborhood and simply waited out her remaining years of living in a racist world, retiring to her bed to "study color."

Morrison creates a memorial to the racial violence of 1874. African Americans were wiped out in some towns. There were eighty-seven lynchings in Kentucky. Colored schools were torched. Like one of the novel's characters, Stamp Paid,[6] we glimpse this violence in the traces left of human life. Stamp Paid finds a small, intimate relic of a child discarded in the aftermath of violence: a red ribbon, "knotted around a curl of wet woolly hair, clinging still to its bit of scalp" (Morrison, 1987, 180). Stunned, dizzy, short of breath, he implores Jesus to explain to him what these people are (Morrison, 1987, 180).[7]

Stamp Paid attempts an answer to this question. He tries to empathize with white folk and see African Americans from their perspective. Stamp Paid wonders whether when white people look at African Americans, they see a jungle full of "swift, unnavigable waters, swinging screaming baboons, sleeping snakes" (Morrison, 1987, 198-99). Stamp Paid knowingly comments that it is the white people themselves who planted the jungle there. In *Playing the Dark*, Morrison suggests that the Euro-Americans who first arrived in America projected onto African Americans the shadow side of their freedom: their experience of being outcasts, their dread of failure, their powerlessness, and their terror of Nature without limits.[8] Racial stereotypes were an attempt to control the unknown. Stereotypes gave Euro-American settlers a simple map with which to navigate the world, particularly aspects of the world which were dangerous.

These psychological explanations help us understand the role of projection in racism, and the ways in which Euro-Americans become disengaged from the humanity of African Americans and at the same time disengaged from the devalued aspects of themselves which they identify with these African Americans. In their attempt to have power over these devalued parts of themselves, they project such qualities onto others. These projections are the result of a potent fusion between distorted images of African Americans and the hateful aspects of themselves. They remain attached at all costs to these distorted images of African Americans and locked in an overpowering stance. Understanding the power dynamics and relational boundaries in racism makes us aware that when we shift into an extreme position of disengagement from and power over aspects of ourselves, and when we project these qualities on others, then violence follows.

THE DISENGAGED AFRICAN AMERICAN COMMUNITY

The community of free Blacks plays an important role in the events leading up to Sethe's murdering her child. They gathered the evening before the murder for a huge feast, prepared by Baby Suggs, Sethe's mother-in-law and the children's grandmother, to celebrate their safe arrival four weeks earlier. The idea for the party occurs to Baby Suggs when Stamp Paid, the generous elderly black man who found Sethe and her newborn, brings two buckets of berries as gifts for the infant. Soon a party is brewing and ninety people gather and feast. The next morning they become furious at what they see as the pride of Baby Suggs. Baby Suggs can smell their disapproval and repulsion toward her for "overstepping." Giving too much is her offense. Concentrating on this, Baby Suggs intuits that there is something else in the air, some danger lurking amidst the smells of disapproval. The danger she smells is the approaching men—Schoolteacher (Sethe's former owner), his nephew, a tracker and the sheriff—who have come to recapture Sethe and her children. Nobody ran on ahead to warn Sethe as they normally would have, because the neighbors are still angry about the excesses of the night before. As soon as she sees her former owner, Sethe gathers her children, flees to the woodshed and kills her not yet two-year-old daughter. Stamp Paid prevents her from killing her second daughter and two sons.

When Sethe is being taken off by the sheriff, the throng of black faces that watch are shocked and also question whether her head was a bit too high, her back too straight. They do not sing, as they usually do. They refuse to wrap her in a cape of singing (Morrison, 1987, 152), which is what they would often do when one of them was captured. The murder and her arrest put an end to Sethe's brief, twenty-eight-day experience of being part of a neighborhood where she is loved, counseled, protected, and fed. Upon her arrest, she feels the community "step back and hold itself at a distance" (Morrison, 1987, 177).

When looked at through the lens of power dynamics and relational boundaries, a central theme emerges concerning the role of the black neighborhood in being an empathic, empowering presence. Such a presence preserves life and sanity amid the overpowering, disengaged, and merged dynamics of racial violence. When the connection between African American individuals and their neighborhood is severed, and those in the neighborhood hold themselves at a distance, then racism and the pain of memories become overwhelming. These intrapsychic dynamics can be studied more closely by looking at the main characters of the novel: those who live at 124 Bluestone Road.

INTRAPSYCHIC DYNAMICS:
WITHIN 124 BLUESTONE ROAD

The novel opens many years after the murder. Sethe and her youngest daughter, Denver, make up a household at number 124 on Bluestone Road. Sethe's two sons have run away, unable to stand the spiteful presence of the ghost. Sethe and Denver, cut off from the community, live in a world unto themselves. Sethe is overwhelmed by a desire to hold on to all of her children, living, dead, and disappeared. Both Sethe and Denver feel a strange attachment to the spiteful ghost, "full of a baby's venom" (Morrison, 1987, 3). Knowing the source of its outrage and how it was too little to understand or even talk about what happened, Sethe remains under the power of the baby's spell, yearning for some way to make her love known to this ghost of a child.

When Sethe remembers the power of her love for this child, a violent memory is evoked. She remembers leaning against a tombstone, "knees wide open as any grave," submitting to ten minutes of coercive sex in exchange for seven engraved letters—the second word, Beloved, of the full inscription she wanted, Dearly Beloved. Whenever Sethe remembers the children she has loved and lost, she must also face memories of overwhelming violence. Though she works hard at not remembering the violence, anything could trigger a memory of the final brutal scenes that occurred before she escaped the Sweet Home farm and her life as a slave.[9]

A figure from the past turns up. It is Paul, one of the men who worked with her husband on the Sweet Home farm eighteen years ago when they were all slaves. Paul is described as the blessed kind of man who allows women to feel their pain and weep about it. In his presence, Sethe cries for the pain of being beaten the night before she ran away eighteen years ago. She cries for the urgency she felt as she ran away. She had to get to her nursing child (the one she later killed) who had gone ahead of her. She cries that "they" "stole" her milk. These are the words she uses to describe the grotesque humiliation of the sexual assault where the white "student" of her slave owner sucked her breasts.

In Paul's presence, Sethe's eighteen-year-old daughter, Denver, weeps for the death of her grandmother, Baby Suggs, nine years earlier. Paul's empathy extends to the ghost, and he feels its sadness soaking him as he walks through its "pool of pulsating red light" where "a kind of weeping clung to the air" (Morrison, 1987, 9, 10). His temporary immersion in this sadness does not overwhelm him. Hours later, the rage of the ghost makes the house pitch from side to side and again Paul is not overwhelmed. Paul is willing to fight the ghost on Sethe's behalf. And the ghost departs for the time being.

Paul's empathic response to these women allows them to feel the pain they have been carrying for years.[10] These moments of empathy cannot be sustained. Both Paul and Sethe have been too deprived of intimacy to stay in such close contact with each other. After being part of a chain gang that slept in cages underground at night, Paul has learned to shut down emotionally, and just exist enough to meet his basic needs of walking toward freedom, eating, sleeping, and singing. Seeing Sethe, he feels his heart spring open. He yearns for a woman who will "gather me. . . . The pieces that I am, she gather them and give them back to me in all the right order" (Morrison, 1987, 273). Paul proposes that the three of them try to make a life together. On a celebratory trip to the carnival, Sethe keeps looking back at their three shadows, which appear to be holding hands—a lovely image for the newfound sense of connection.

Paul's presence makes Sethe aware of how much she has been deadened to the world around her and to her own feelings. Emotions long buried come quickly to the surface. Whereas before his arrival everything seemed drab, now heat feels hot. Marveling at suddenly noticing colors, she wonders whether she stopped "remembering" colors after she saw the red baby blood and the pink gravestone. The way in which she has shut out colors from her awareness depicts her level of disengagement from the world around her. Colors are a symbol not only of engagement, but also of empowerment, when empowerment is thought of as fullness of being.

The delicate beginnings of transformation for Sethe and Paul are still germinating when a young woman arrives. She is nineteen or twenty. No one sees her walk fully dressed out of the river. We are given many clues that she is odd. She has new skin: "lineless and smooth" (Morrison, 1987, 51). For the first day she does little more than sleep and drink large quantities of water. She says her name is Beloved, and she gives no sign of having had any life before she arrived on their doorstep. She has an insatiable appetite for anything sweet. She also has an insatiable appetite for Sethe's presence—her voice, her smells, her sounds: "Sethe was licked, tasted, eaten by Beloved's eyes" (Morrison, 1987, 57). When Beloved touches her, Sethe feels the heaviness of Beloved's desire. When Sethe begins to tell her stories, this becomes a way of feeding Beloved. Sethe has avoided talking with anybody about her past because it is too painful, yet she finds a strange pleasure in telling Beloved these stories.

Even before Paul realizes who Beloved is, he compares her presence to the ghost. He says to himself that it wasn't hard for him to "beat up" a ghost, but he couldn't bring himself to evict a "colored girl" from the house into the hostile territory ruled by the Klan (Morrison, 1987, 66). Paul realizes that Beloved is physically moving him, letting him sleep in one place in the house, then making it impossible for him to sleep there. He feels helpless about preventing this. Beloved is an overpowering presence in the household.

When a neighbor in the community makes Paul aware of the story of Sethe and her murdered infant, Paul wants Sethe to explain the murder. She tries to. She describes how she experienced the freedom of Cincinnati as a freedom to love whomever she wanted. For Sethe, this freedom to love becomes a freedom to kill her children in order to keep them safe. She sees herself as having the power to act in this way. Describing the murder of her daughter, she says she wanted to put her children somewhere where they would be safe. Paul says her love is "too thick"[11] and remarks that Sethe doesn't realize "where the world stopped and she began" (Morrison, 1987, 164). This is how Paul describes the fusion between Sethe and her children. He is sharply aware not only of Sethe's fusion but of her overpowering love, which compels her to violent actions. Though she talks like any other woman about babies, "what she meant could cleave the bone" (Morrison, 1987, 164) because for Sethe a handsaw is the way to safety. According to Sethe, a love that makes her kill her children to save them from what is terrible is the fullest extension of love a mother can have. For Paul this is the basest sort of motherly love, an animal and not a human love. At this point of disagreement, a huge gulf opens up between them.

During this exchange, Paul focuses on Sethe's outrageous love, and "forgets" that he wanted to confess his secret of having sex with Beloved in the coldhouse where he sleeps. Paul leaves 124 Bluestone Road; and Sethe, Denver, and Beloved descend into a maelstrom world of their own.

The second part of the novel opens with Sethe's discovery that Beloved is her child returned from the dead—a discovery she makes when she hears Beloved humming a song that Sethe made up and sang to her children. Sethe smiles because she will now be able to lay down the burden of remembering everything for her dead or lost children. Remembering was a way of staying connected with her children, keeping a lifeline between them and her.

Sethe becomes even more deeply enmeshed in her own world and disconnected from the community. Now that Beloved has returned, Sethe thinks "there is no world outside my door" (Morrison, 1987, 184). Sethe also believes that Beloved remembers and understands everything—that they are fused in this way. In her daughter's presence, she remembers her longing and searching for her own mother, after her mother was hanged when she was a young child. Sethe spends endless time playing games with Beloved and loses her job. She constantly feeds Beloved and becomes rail thin while Beloved grows "bigger, plumper by the day" (Morrison, 1987, 239). Morrison is describing the extreme overpowering needs of a two-year-old who is locked in merger with her mother. Mother and child have lost even a sense of physical boundaries between them. Sethe feeds Beloved as a way of feeding herself. When Sethe momentarily tries to shift the power imbalance and regain her role as "the unquestioned mother whose word is law," Beloved becomes violent (Morrison, 1987, 240).[12]

The sweet charmed relationship between mother and child begins to turn sour and malevolent. Beloved's demands increase, and with them Sethe's compliance. The demands become accusations: how could Sethe have left her? Even though Sethe is utterly exhausted and drained, she remains "locked in a love that wore everyone out" (Morrison, 1987, 243).

Denver is able to stand outside of the overpowering merger of Sethe and Beloved. She realizes that she must venture outside the world of her home for the first time in ten years to ask for help. She seeks out a neighbor and haltingly asks for food. Her one request for food is communicated throughout the neighborhood, and soon baskets of food are left in front of her house. When Denver describes Beloved as a cousin come to visit, the women in the neighborhood realize at once that Sethe's dead daughter "had come back to fix her" (Morrison, 1987, 255). They decide that it's time to launch a rescue operation. One of the women understands Beloved's presence as "sin moving on in the house, unleashed and sassy" (Morrison, 1987, 256). The black women plan on confronting this ghost and arrive in a crowd of thirty. Standing in front of the house, they begin hollering, a sound without words, searching "for the right combination, the key, the code, the sound that broke the back of words" (Morrison, 1987, 261). Amid this wave of sound, a white man arrives in his wagon to pick up Denver for work. To Sethe it is Schoolteacher, coming to get her child. Sethe runs toward the white man, ice pick in raised hand, trying to reach him to kill him. The women wrestle her to the ground and knock her out.

Afterward, huddled under a bright quilt, singing to herself, Sethe seems to be lost. When Paul returns, she opens her eyes and sees again that blessedness in Paul which allows her to reconnect with her own feelings. The story ends in a moment of tenderness between them.

THEOLOGICAL REFLECTIONS

African American literature that retells the stories of racial violence highlights what happens during the extreme dynamics of disengagement, merger, and power over others. We can see that Euro-American men and women remain in a disengaged stance, unable to experience the most basic form of empathy, that of seeing African Americans as human beings. In the process of disengagement, African American people are equated with and reduced to functions they have in a racist society: black men as laborers, black women as nurturers, procreators, and sexual objects. The Euro-Americans have an intense need to keep these African Americans in their "place": locked in the functions they perform, locked in stereotypes, locked within a system that deprives them of their humanity. In racism, disengagement and merger work together with a need to overpower. The consequences of racism are seen in the physical and sexual violence that is recounted over and over again throughout many African American novels. Daily life is filled with rape and beatings. Family genograms are saturated with murders and suicides.

Even in the midst of such violence, God is experienced as a sustaining presence. In Morrison's *Beloved,* the best of her characters, when confronted with the worst brutality, invoke God's name. This is done not in anger toward God, but in appeal. Amy, a young white woman fleeing from poverty and servitude, cares for Sethe when she is pregnant and on the run. When she sees how Sethe's back has been "laid open" with a beating, she exclaims, "Come here, Jesus"—a heartfelt invocation. Amy describes Sethe's horrible wounds as a tree in bloom, and she wonders aloud what in the world God has in mind. Then, telling Sethe to thank her Maker that Amy came along, she gets to work, healing Sethe in the only way she knows how, by draping her back with palmfuls of spiderwebs.

When Stamp Paid, the aged man who has ferried people to free-dom and been a father and grandfather to the whole neighborhood, finds a red ribbon tied around a curl of wet woolly hair, he suddenly feels overwhelmed by the brutality he has known and touched; tasted, seen, heard, and smelled for years. He asks Jesus to tell him what these people are. He carries the ribbon with him in the days that follow, and is driven to reconnect with Sethe and bring the community back around her.

Both of these characters, when confronted with the brutality of slavery, invoke the name of Jesus, then get down to work in ways that are empowering and empathic. They become part of a transformative process rooted in the name of Jesus.[13]

Morrison has used Romans 9:25 (KJV) as an epigraph to *Beloved*: "I will call them my people, which were not my people; and her beloved, which was not beloved." In the context of the Letter to the Romans, these verses refer to the Gentile people, who have been despised and outcast. God will claim them as children of the living God. The tenderness of these verses reflects God's love for the despised and outcast.

The last pages of the novel speak of a "loneliness that can't be rocked . . . that roams" (Morrison, 1987, 274), and the spirit of Be-loved, which now becomes "disremembered and unaccounted for, she cannot be lost because no one is looking for her" (Morrison, 1987,

274). No human being can love her and remember her as she needed to be loved and remembered. When Sethe tried, she became over-powered and consumed. The opening words of the novel, its epigraph, remind us that she is one of God's beloved. We cannot love her as God can, for when we try to, we become consumed in her rage and desire. And so we must let go and care for the living.

Morrison underlines that such caring for the living must be done in community. In *Beloved* she portrays the destruction that comes when a family isolates itself from its community and tries to bear and repair the pain inflicted by racism. Cut off from the community, Baby Suggs, Sethe, and Denver become immersed in the pain, not only of those they have loved, but of all who have been lost and abandoned in the wreckage of racism. This is symbolized by the ring of voices that surrounds Sethe's house. Approaching the house, Stamp Paid can hear this "pack of haunts" from the road (Morrison, 1987, 170). He knows that he has to lean on the power of Jesus Christ because he is dealing with spirits that are "older but not stronger" than Jesus himself (Morrison, 1987, 173). The first time he tries to penetrate this circle of voices, he hears "a conflagration of hasty voices—loud, urgent, all speaking at once" (Morrison, 1987, 172). The only word he can make out is the word "mine." The second time he approaches the house, he hears these voices differently. He still can't understand what they are saying, but he envisions them as "the people of the broken necks, of fire-cooked blood and black girls who had lost their ribbons" (Morrison, 1987, 181).

A single mother, no matter how "thick" her love, cannot contain the pain of even her own lost child, let alone the pain of all of these lost children. When she tries, as Sethe does, she becomes exhausted, depleted, and caught in the rage and desire of her child. Her neighbors save her: Stamp Paid and the band of women arrive to exorcise the spirit. James Baldwin lyrically describes this need for community:

> Generations do not cease to be born, and we are responsible to them because we are the only witnesses they have. The sea rises, the light fails, lovers cling to each other, and children cling to us. The moment we cease to hold each other, the moment we break faith with one another, the sea engulfs us and the light goes out. (Baldwin, quoted in Morrison, 1992, 196)

Morrison's novel *Beloved* elaborates the complexity of what clinging to each other means. When such clinging happens in parent-child and lover relationships in which one is cut off from one's community, then the "sea engulfs us and the light goes out." The "holding" must be done, not by individuals, but within the context of community.

Morrison wants to reclaim the empowering role of the community, and this theme is sounded throughout her novels. *Sula,* an earlier novel, opens thus: "In that place, where they tore the night shade and blackberry patches from their roots to make room for the Medallion City Golf Course, there was once a neighborhood" (Morrison, 1974, 1). Morrison uses the word *neighborhood* rather than *community:*

> My tendency is to focus on neighborhoods and communities. And the community, the black community—I don't like to use that term be-cause it came to mean something very much different in the sixties and seventies, as though we had to forge one—but it had seemed to me that it was always there, only we called it the "neighborhood." And there was this life-giving, very, very strong sustenance that people got from the neighborhood. (Morrison, in an interview with Stepto, 1993, 379)

Besides the role of the community, Morrison highlights the role of faith in confronting and not being broken by racial violence. Stamp Paid arms himself with his faith before he steps into the maelstrom of wailing voices surrounding Sethe's house. Ella, another neighbor, becomes convinced that the women must rescue Sethe and Denver. She uses the image of unbounded sin to describe the dynamics going on within the house, between Sethe and Beloved. These neighbors continually draw upon their faith and their sense of a God who is continually at hand.

PASTORAL THEOLOGICAL REFLECTIONS

> Slavery as a subject continues to hold a particular fascination at least in part because it provides the ground upon which writers of critical and imaginative literature alike may investigate an array of issues that are pressing in contemporary culture. (Valerie Smith, 1993, 342-343)

When we view Morrison's portrayal of slavery and the time of Reconstruction in terms of power dynamics and relational bounda-ries, several themes emerge: the violence of racial stereotypes, the sustaining role of the neighborhood, the consequences of isolation from one's neighborhood, and the need for a faith that can sustain one in the midst of violence. These themes resonate with contemporary problems in American culture.

Racial stereotypes, once used by settlers leaving home and journeying into a strange new world, are still used to deal with the feelings of being overpowered by an economic and social system where many people feel alienated from one another. A vivid illustration of this is Robert Altman's chilling film, *Short Cuts* (a compilation of the short stories of Raymond Carver). The film opens with a trio of planes taking off to blanket a city with insecticide. We are introduced to the various couples and families portrayed in the film as they notice the buzz of the airplanes and the fine mist of insecticide. Although their lives are interwoven at various moments throughout the film, in haphazard and ominous ways, the only event that they experience together in the film is this misting of the city. The sense of all of these people being contaminated by something in the air unfolds throughout the movie, as we watch the covert and overt violence and neglect that is part of all of their lives. For the most part, they are caught in vicious power struggles with their lovers, spouses, and children that result in physical, emotional, and sexual violence. The death of a young child in a hit-and-run accident, the murder of a young woman whose naked body is found in a river, and the suicide of a promising young musician depict the casualties of this culture. For most of the film the characters are numb to the violence in their lives—both the violence they experience and the violence they enact. There are very few moments in the film where its characters can feel one another's pain.

When we compare Altman's film *Short Cuts* to Morrison's novel, we see the same dynamics: intense power struggles in which people are merged in roles and stereotypes that keep them disengaged from one another. The trio of insecticide-spraying planes at the film's beginning and end become an ominous image of a malevolent God—a technology that is supposed to be protecting the city but instead seems to be blanketing it with poison. Morrison's comment about racial stereotypes can be expanded to describe the culture portrayed by Raymond Carver and Robert Altman: "In a society with a history of trying to accommodate both slavery and freedom, and a present that wishes both to exploit and deny the pervasiveness of racism, black people are rarely individualized" (Morrison, 1992, xiv-xv).

Altman's film portrays the slavery enacted in family violence where all are caught in vicious power struggles. The pull toward merger and disengagement makes individualization extraordinarily difficult. There is a poignant moment of such individualization in the film. A mother and father whose son has just died in a hit-and-run accident track down an angry baker. He has been pestering them at all hours with crank calls about their son's birthday cake, which his mother ordered and then forgot to pick up after the accident. The parents barge into his bakery in the early hours of the morning and confront him. The confrontation becomes a way for their rage at their son's death to finally erupt. The mean-eyed baker serves as a fitting target. As he takes in their anger and grief, he becomes gentle, helping them to sit down, offering them warm bread and rolls, and coaxing them to eat, reminding them that eating is a small, good thing in a time like this. This scene (taken from Carver's moving story, "A small good thing") is one of the few moments of empathy in the film. Throughout most of the film, characters are unable to experience one another as individuals. The other is seen in terms of stereotypes, which inevitably involve disengagement from the other's humanity and merger in the form of projections upon the other.

Cornel West has described contemporary American life in the following terms:

> Never before has the seductive market way of life held such sway in nearly every sphere of American life. This market way of life promotes addictions to stimulation and obsessions with comfort and convenience. . . . The common denominator is a rugged individualism and rapacious hedonism in quest of a perennial "high" in body and mind. (West in Morrison, 1992, 399)

Many commentators on post-modern culture note its rampant or rugged individualism (Borgmann, 1992; Taylor, 1991). The term *individualism* implies isolation and disengagement. What this term does not communicate is the ways in which people remain caught in power struggles that dehumanize and result in violence. This is a form of slavery that continues today. When we compare Morrison's novel *Beloved* to Altman's cinematic interweaving of Raymond Carver's stories, we might wonder whether the roots of American culture in the brutality of slavery make it more likely than some post-modern cultures to remain caught in power struggles that dehumanize others and lead to hatred and violence.

In *Beloved* Morrison depicts the central role of faith in surviving racial violence, and how faith energizes individuals and the neighborhood to survive and work toward healing. Ed Wimberly (1984, 1991), Archie Smith, Jr. (1982, 1987), and James Evans (1990) have suggested that African American Christianity continues to offer a means of surviving the violence that results from being caught in intense power struggles that dehumanize. Evans argues that African American Christianity, with its history of "not fitting" in a modern culture, may be carrying within its history the seeds of a post-modern faith. Three aspects of African American Christianity—in particular its models of care and healing—make it an alternative "to mainline theologies and psychologies which uphold the private, autonomous and self-contained individual as the North American ideal" (Smith, 1987, 174). When one focuses on the individual as "private, autonomous and self-contained," one loses sight of the ways in which people enmeshed in power struggles form distorted images of themselves and others which result in hatred and violence.

First, African American Christianity has a long history of "prophetic critique against a society and the modernist spirit that could justify kidnapping, slavery, exploitation, and racism in the name of religion" (Evans, 1990, 218). Their critique has been rooted in both their experiences of dehumanization in a racist culture and their knowledge that they were beloved by God. African American Christianity can prophetically suggest ways to navigate our way through the collapse of the modern culture.

The second way in which African American Christian tradition provides seeds for a post-modern faith is through its rootedness in stories of the faithful. Historically, African American theology has grown out of stories of African American Christians (Wilmore, 1983; Wilmore and Cone, 1979). "The real shapers of black theology are the unknown and unsung saints and sinners who daily live out the meaning of their embodied faith in Jesus" (Smith, 1987, 178). More recently, African Americans have drawn upon African American literature to elaborate their ethics and theology (Evans, 1987; Williams, 1985; Cannon, 1985, 1988).[14] The theology embodied in stories of the faithful and African American literature are models of post-modern theologies. Drawing upon the writings of Stephen Toulmin, Walter Brueggemann has suggested that in the shift from modernity to post-modernity, we see a move "from written to oral, universal to particular, general to local, and timeless to timely" (Brueggemann 1993, 6). A post-modern faith values the particular, the local, and the timely, and this is what an African American theology based on stories and literature does. Black pastoral theologies reflect this valuing of stories as a source of healing and transformation within individuals, families, communities, and indeed the culture (Wimberly, 1991, 1992).

The third way in which African American theology is post-modern is in making relationality and community central to its theology. Archie Smith, Jr. (1987) draws upon Bernard Loomer's metaphor of the Web to describe an African American understanding of the relationship between God and world. The themes of the inseparability of God and world and the importance of relationality are central to Toni Morrison's *Beloved*. The centrality of community and relational life are values that have been lost in a modern culture in which we remain disengaged from one another's humanity and simultaneously caught in power struggles that generate distorted images of who we and others are. The assumption of positivistic science, that we can step outside of our world, predict and control it, has made us not only "expatriates" who "live in self-imposed exile from communal conversation and action" (Borgmann, 1992, 3) but also people caught in webs of dehumanization and violence. In reclaiming the centrality of community, we need to beware of the dangers of becoming merged within the community and losing ourselves in collectivism (Evans, 1987). Collectivism in which neither the individual nor the good of the whole society is valued can lead to an unbalanced political system, with an adversarial spirit:

> in which citizen efficacy consists in being able to get your rights, whatever the consequences for the whole. Both judicial retrieval [where more and more of American law and politics is focused on maintaining or reversing judicial decisions][15] and single-issue politics [e.g., issues like abortion] operate from this stance and further strengthen it. (Taylor, 1991, 117)

The challenge is to maintain communities where power energizes relationships and is life-giving, not for individuals[16] or even particular communities, but for the good of the whole.

Wimberly (1979) has pointed out that the pastoral care offered within African American communities has consisted primarily of sustaining: "helping persons courageously and creatively endure and transcend" racism (Wimberly, 1979, 18). Healing was made enormously difficult "because oppression made wounds almost irreparable" (Wimberly, 1979, 38). Wimberly notes that Euro-American models of pastoral care have focused on healing individuals through one-to-one relationships where there is an assumption that one's family, community, and culture were benevolent. Morrison's novel *Beloved* and Altman's film *Short Cuts* illustrate the malevolence of our society and its centuries of violence. The task of the church as a whole is to transform the violent culture in which we all move, live, and have our being. Without cultural transformation, pastoral care cannot move beyond sustaining those who endure the overpowering, disengaged, and merged dynamics of our culture.

CHAPTER THREE

LIFE-GIVING SEXUAL AND SPIRITUAL DESIRE

The novels by Updike, Ross, and Morrison describe people caught in the extremes of overpowering, merged, and disengaged dynamics. In two of these novels (*A Month of Sundays* and *As for Me and My House*) there seems little hope of intrapsychic change, and at the novels' end we are left wondering whether more abuse or neglect will occur. In one of these novels, Toni Morrison's *Beloved,* there is no change in the overpowering, merged, and disengaged dynamics of the racist society she portrays. While we are left with some hope that the novel's characters may be able to sustain themselves in the midst of racial violence, we are not given any hope that there will be societal transformation.

Using these three novels to create case studies highlights what happens during power struggles involving disengagement and merger. These novels illustrate abuse and neglect and not healing. Indeed, they highlight how difficult any movement toward healing is when such extreme merged, disengaged, and overpowering dynamics are present. We are left with no illusions that transformation is easy.

I have chosen the story of Anne Clavidge, who is one of about six complex characters in the novel *Nuns and Soldiers* by Iris Murdoch, as a case study of intrapsychic transformation in a social context where those around her remain disengaged from her humanity and merged with their images of her as a nun. The most touching aspects of this transformation concern her relationship with God. I know of few contemporary novels that illustrate the complexity and profundity of post-modern faith in the way this novel does. By post-modern faith, I mean a faith in which we let go of a two-tiered worldview (of an overpowering God up above) and our certainty that we can know and define God, and at the same time we experience a profoundly intimate relationship with this God we cannot know. This is Anne's struggle throughout the novel. As I shall illustrate, one way to understand her struggle is in terms of moving from disengagement, merger, and overpowering dynamics to empathy and empowerment. This novel illustrates the intrapsychic transformation possible when empathy and empowerment are present, and it specifically describes the transformation of faith and one's relationship with God.

This novel is set for the most part in England. Its cast of characters fall into two socio-economic classes: those who are highly educated, cultured, and wealthy, and those who have struggled to get an education, realize ambitions (particularly artistic ambitions), and survive financially.[1] All of the characters except one are British Caucasians; the exception is an immigrant from Poland. Anne Clavidge, while aligned with the upper class because of her education and culture, is not wealthy and indeed seeks a deliberately frugal lifestyle.

THE STORY OF ANNE CLAVIDGE

When Anne begins university, she leaves behind the innocent, cloistered childhood and adolescence of growing up in all-girl boarding schools and enters "a carnival, a maelstrom, a festival of popularity and personality and sex" (Murdoch, 1980, 60). As an undergraduate she explores her emerging sexuality and devotes most of her energy to love affairs which she pursues in secrecy. When graduation draws closer, Anne experiences a great choice looming ahead of her. She converts to Catholicism and then takes religious vows. As she says, religious vows are a way to regain her innocence and safeguard it, and she associates this innocence with God. She wants nothing more than to "float free" of "worldly thoughts."

She appears to be perfectly suited for a life of contemplative prayer, in that the routines of the convent's devotional life increase her delight, deepen her joy, and become as simple as breathing. Amidst this increasing intimacy with God, a turning point gradually emerges. She begins to feel as though she is in the wrong place. The fluttering of anxiety feels like a small symptom heralding a serious illness or some immense bodily transformation.

There was, however, "no revelation . . . It was under a negative and agnostic sign that she must now proceed" (Murdoch, 1980, 66). In this lack of a positive revelation,[2] she struggles to name who God is for her and to see where she must go next. All she knows, with growing certainty, is that she must leave, and leave with the consent and blessing of her mother superior. Anne's leave-taking from the convent is a slow process that she and her superior move through together. Her superior gives her an image of herself "as a secret anchoress." Anne envisions herself as "one of God's spies, the spy of a non-existent God" (Murdoch, 1980, 67). While her sense of who God is remains a negation, she experiences Christ as "her Christ, the only one that was really hers" (Murdoch, 1980, 67).

Upon leaving her order, she joins her friend Gertrude and ends up staying with her through the imminent death of Gertrude's husband, Guy. Initially, she feels strange and frozen, except for some moments with Guy, in which she draws close to him as he speaks of dying and what lay beyond death. She yearns for the silences and routines of the convent. She begins reading novels, something she has not done since she entered her religious order. She finds such reading both marvelous and too much, and is overwhelmed by the excessive details and intensity of what she reads.

She still prays continually, but instead of it being as natural as breathing, praying seems like "the strange awful breathing of a body kept alive after the brain is dead" (Murdoch, 1980, 67). She wonders whether this "anaesthetic numbness" is permanent, or whether it is the prelude to some change of being. She pictures a creature, curled up and half buried, which wakes up in great pain to find itself being transformed into something new. She wonders if she is about to undergo some sort of metamorphosis.

After Gertrude's husband dies, Anne becomes a companion to Gertrude, seeing the immediate task ahead of her as caring for her grieving friend. The two of them get away from London for several days, staying at a cottage on the ocean. While walking along the beach, Gertrude reminds Anne that Anne used to be a "demon" swimmer. Anne replies that she thought she would never swim again. Though the sea is cold and rough, Gertrude teasingly suggests that Anne swim now, and Anne takes this as a dare. Anne drags off her clothes and dives in with an intense, acute hunger that shoots through her like a piercing sexual desire. Her swim turns from joyful exuberant mastery to an exhaustive struggle toward the shore as she feels the overwhelming power of the waves. After a harrowing attempt to get close enough to shore to stand up, she is rescued by Gertrude, who plunges in and pulls her friend to safety. Later, Gertrude and Anne laugh about the sight of Anne, clothed with nothing but a cross around her neck.

In the weeks that follow, Anne shifts from experiencing herself as frozen, with a dead body, to feeling invisible to the men she now meets. One of the most intriguing themes in this novel is the extent to which our roles define our sexual desire and that these roles are forced upon us by others. So Anne is forced by those around her to remain a nun, and with this role to keep her sexual desires invisible. As she experiences the pain of her metamorphosis, impelled by new sexual and spiritual desires, there is no one to help her name her pain and consolidate a new sexual and spiritual identity. Quite the opposite happens, when the men around her refuse to see or name any metamorphosis ("Once a nun, always a nun!"). No wonder she pictures her unfolding sexual desire as impelling her toward some radical break in her identity: a winged beast, entirely different, even living in a different element.

Her friend Gertrude teasingly describes her as Mary Magdalene in reverse, and encourages her to wear jewelry other than a small cross. Anne finds this image pleasing. She starts to notice how she looks and realizes with surprise that she is good-looking and still quite young. She feels "old appetites stirring." When she realizes that her friend Gertrude has begun an affair with a young man, Anne is once again overcome with "a feeling of the horribleness and dangerousness of life . . . like a sudden nausea. This was the warmth, the mess, which she had fled from to the convent" (Murdoch, 1980, 248).

After this event of her friend falling in love, an extraordinary thing happens. Jesus Christ appears to Anne in a vision.[3] This is a strangely comic visitation, made humorous by Murdoch's descriptions of Jesus' appearance. He is pale, but not with a numinous, heavenly pallor; it is as if he has been deprived of light, like a fish that has lived in the depths of the sea, or "a grub inside a fruit"! He is wearing plimsolls (a British term for running shoes) and seems somewhat disheveled. In spite of these comic, even grotesque qualities, he is beautiful, and Anne wants to cling to him.[4] When her finger brushes his clothing, she feels a sting and sees a deep burn.[5] She can't bear him to leave her and he gives her a small gray stone, a little chipped at one end—as modest in appearance as her strange visitor. While pressing her burnt finger against the hard, cold stone, she declares that there is no God, but that Christ lives, her Christ, "her nomadic, cosmic Christ, uniquely hers, focused upon her alone by all the rays of being" (1980, 500).

She resumes her ordinary life, except now it is extraordinary. She also names, for the first time, that something has happened to her. She has fallen in love with a friend of Gertrude, someone nicknamed the Count. Though the Count is part of this novel from its very beginning, we do not find out that his real name is Peter until Anne falls in love and begins calling him by his name. When we go back in the story to find out more about who the Count is, we learn that he was befriended first by Guy, Gertrude's husband. When he is introduced to the friends of Gertrude and her husband, Guy, they ask, "Where did Guy dig up our Count?" and "Whatever was he doing before *we* discovered him?" His role is that of a gentleman, and his particular dignity and diligence in fulfilling his duties give him a soldierly air.

Anne experiences her love as an illness, made terrible by the fact that "Peter still saw her as a nun . . . a holy woman, innocent, calm, untouchable, and chaste" (Murdoch, 1980, 304). Anne wants to smash this image and realizes that she could do this in two seconds by simply declaring her love. She is afraid that he would "recoil in horror, disgust—pity" (Murdoch, 1980, 304). Instead of declaring her love, she decides to wait for him to fully see her. When the Count contemplates suicide, saying that he doesn't believe in God, Anne tells him that his life doesn't belong to him: "Our being spreads out far beyond us and mingles with the beings of others. We live in other people's thoughts, in their plans, in their dreams. This is as if there were God. We have an infinite responsibility" (Murdoch, 1980, 454).[6]

Her waiting for the Count to fully see her is shattered when her friend Gertrude, now married to her young lover, wants the Count to love her as a devotee. Gertrude draws him into her circle. She teasingly makes a love treaty with him and suggests that he be her attendant soldier. Peter accepts this limited role. Anne realizes she has lost Peter—he is forever the Count. He is not able himself to step out of the role into which Gertrude casts him.

Though Gertrude herself named Anne as Mary Magdalene in reverse—an image quickly internalized by Anne—Gertrude remains unaware of Anne's love for the Count. In binding the Count to herself, Gertrude thinks that she has created a perfect world which she likens to a sheepfold, with all of the sheep gathered in (Murdoch, 1980, 474) or, as Anne says, a playpen with all the children in it (1980, 467). She tries to draw Anne into her circle as well. When Anne is determined to go away, Gertrude at first orders her to stay, telling her that they will be a happy family. Then Gertrude begs Anne to stay, saying she can't do without her. Gertrude can make sense of Anne's determination to depart only by telling herself that Anne is still a nun. She tries to convince Anne to be *her* nun (Murdoch, 1980, 477). Gertrude remains deeply wounded by Anne's "defection."

Anne does not lose herself by settling for some false consolation by becoming Gertrude's "nun" and entering the sheepfold Gertrude creates. In this she remains true to the nomadic, cosmic Christ that is uniquely hers and true to her vision of being interconnected in a web that spreads far beyond her. This infinite web of responsibility is her way of describing the "as-if" God.

The novel closes on the eve of her departure to America. As she looks upward the abundantly falling snow, illuminated by street lamps, reminds her of something: "It looked like the heavens spread out in glory, totally unrolled before the face of God, countless, limitless, eternally beautiful, the universe in majesty proclaiming the presence and the goodness of its Creator" (Murdoch, 1980, 511).

COMMENTS

In Anne's story we hear the ways in which spiritual and sexual passion are intertwined. Her spiritual transformation goes hand in hand with newly unfolding sexual passions. This is an important theme in Murdoch's novels. She understands Eros to be "a mediating spirit that takes human desire beyond the sexual to the good. For while passion can bind, it can also liberate and lead, and can ultimately be purified" (Tucker, 1992, 8). Murdoch is highly sensitive to the potential for sexual passion to become a desire for power over and merger. Falling in love, as she illustrates in novel after novel, can make us "derealize the other, devour and absorb him, subject him to the mechanism of our own fantasy" (Murdoch, 1977, 36). In *Nuns and*

71

Soldiers, Anne Clavidge avoids the usual fate of Murdoch's characters who fall in love. Instead of becoming obsessed with the Count, her erotic energy eventually leads her beyond the Count to God.

In *Nuns and Soldiers,* Murdoch illustrates how much our sexuality is shaped by the roles into which we cast ourselves and are cast by others. The constriction of these roles is associated here with the image of home. Throughout the novel, Anne returns over and over again to the question of what home means. She is aware that she left the convent because it was a home. Several times she recalls the saying that foxes have holes but the Son of Man had nowhere to lay his head. While we might use the word *home* to describe an empathic, empowering environment, for Anne home is associated with merged, overpowering dynamics. Home is a configuration of roles that becomes rigid and confining. In this sense, home constricts and limits fullness of being, both sexually and spiritually. Elizabeth Dipple, in a commentary on *Nuns and Soldiers,* says Murdoch rejects "at-homeness in the world" and depicts it as a powerful, even overwhelming force which "distract[s] attention from the true centre" (Dipple, 1982, 310).[7]

> The at-homeness and warmth which the bourgeois world longs for and tries so energetically to obtain are opposed to death, to the task of Christ, to the cosmos itself . . . The opposition of the reality of cosmic homelessness to the bourgeois longing for at-homeness is one of Murdoch's major themes in *Nuns and Soldiers.* (Dipple, 1982, 312)

I also hear in this story how much our spirituality is shaped by the roles into which we cast God. Anne is remarkable in her tolerance of ambiguity: her belief in what is not revealed—the negative, agnostic sign and the "as-if" God. What comes out of this openness to God's being are some lyrical apprehensions of who God is: this vision of our beings spread out far beyond us and mingling with others, and the closing vision of the universe in majesty proclaiming the presence and goodness of the "as-if" God. The sign of the small, chipped stone given to her in her vision opens up a vast horizon of her own potentiality: "the stone in whose compass her Visitor had made her see the Universe, everything that is" (Murdoch, 1980, 507). She is like the small chipped stone. It becomes "an image of the tiny particular which is everything. . . . For contemporary Anne it means that total attention must be paid to the pointless particular, and that such attention is incomprehensible but significant" (Dipple, 1982, 330).

Dipple reminds us that another character, Hugo in Murdoch's first novel, *Under the Net,* says, "God is a task. God is detail. It all lies close to your hand" (Murdoch, 1954, 258). Anne can appreciate both that the work is hers to do, and that she is infinitely connected with others. As Rita Nakashima Brock says:

> No one else can stop the suffering of brokenheartedness in our world but our own courage and willingness to act in the midst of the awareness of our own fragility. . . . Our heartfelt action, not alone, but in the fragile resilient interconnections we share with others, generates the power that makes and sustains life. (Brock, 1991, 106)

The novels of Updike, Ross, and Morrison illustrate the abuse that follows when overpowering, merged, and disengaged dynamics abound in intrapsychic, interpersonal, communal, and cultural systems. In using two novels about clergy who become sexually involved with parishioners, I have looked specifically at the abuse that follows when clergy either wander into sexual relationships because of feeling overpowered, or act in sexually violent ways because of an intense desire to have power over others. These case studies of disengaged, merged, and overpowering dynamics and the abuse that follows illustrate what happens when we wittingly or unwittingly cross the line between thoughts and actions. As I will suggest in the following chapters, we all experience the dynamics of disengagement, merger, and power imbalances. It is crucial that we take care of others, ourselves, and God's creation by monitoring these dynamics in our selves, our families, communities, and culture, and remaining vigilant to the ways in which these dynamics shape our thoughts, words, and actions. When vigilance lapses, abuse or neglect is likely to occur if we cross the boundary between thoughts and actions.

CHAPTER FOUR

POWER DYNAMICS IN PASTORAL CARE AND COUNSELING

We of the ministering professions shall not be delivered from evil. But we can learn to deal with it.[1]

A CIRCULAR MODEL OF POWER DYNAMICS

When I was clinically trained in family systems theory a decade ago, I understood power dynamics as circular, with everyone in a family or church system sharing, giving up, or taking power within the system. Power was a commodity to which everyone had equal access. Wearing "systems glasses" allowed me to see how the frail elderly parent, seemingly the weakest member of the family system, could actually be at the helm of the boat, steering it on its course. In a small rural parish, I could see that the most important decisions about worship and the church school were often made by the all-female choir as they robed for worship every Sunday, not by the all-male session who met six times a year. With a systems perspective, I no longer saw power as something static and fixed by a person's place in a hierarchy.

The trouble with this perspective was that I no longer saw the power hierarchies that did accord people power over others because of their gender, race, or socioeconomic status.[2] I no longer saw such power hierarchies because the cultural context was blurred and out of focus when I scrutinized the church family or an individual family. I remember how one member of the congregation, a young woman my own age, would ask questions about my stipend every year at the annual meeting, implying that the minimum stipend I received was actually worth more because of all the "tax breaks" I received. I puzzled over these questions in terms of the extended family of which she was a part, and how her questions figured in the power struggles of the church system. Looking back on this now, I wonder more about what her own situation as a woman was. What educational and professional opportunities did she have? What was the quality of her life? How easy was it for her to leave home as a single woman? How easy was it for her to develop intimate relationships within a small community? Previously, I had seen her as a cog in a family and church system. Now I wondered to what extent her life and her questions of me were shaped by her gender, her culture, and her socioeconomic class.

Perhaps it's not surprising that I could so easily blur power imbalances created by race, gender, and class, since often I was the one afforded power by such imbalances. I am a Caucasian American-Canadian and grew up in a middle-class home. I received the education I wanted and I have never been without such basic necessities as medical insurance, a home, and food. As such, I have never experienced racial discrimination, chronic financial hardship, or limitations in my choice of vocation. I have experienced sexual violence and have known the world to be a dangerous, life-threatening place. This experience of violence has made vivid to me what it is like to be overpowered.

Being overpowered can threaten our lives emotionally, spiritually, or physically. It is a more common experience than we usually acknowledge. Acknowledging experiences of being overpowered is painful because it undermines our most basic beliefs: that the world is a safe place, that those who love us (including God) will protect us from all harm, and that we will always be able to think, talk, or fight our way out of dangerous situations. If we are fortunate, we will not experience being overpowered until we are old enough to make sense of such experiences in whatever ways we can.

Our tendency to deny our own experiences of being overpowered makes us want to believe that power is something to which we all have equal access. This belief supports a circular understanding of power. I find it intriguing that family systems theory took shape during the 1950s in pioneering clinical work with people diagnosed as schizophrenic. At the time (and still to some extent today) schizophrenia was viewed as the least treatable of mental illnesses— the illness simply overpowered the individual and erased any sense of his or her ability to work and love as a fulfilled human being. During the fifties, the medical model of schizophrenia was individualistic and biological. Systems family therapists began to move beyond this model by suggesting that schizophrenia had to do with family relationships and with the quality of family interactions—particularly power struggles. Their interventions were designed to dismantle the crazy-making double binds in which parents put their schizophrenic son or daughter. Pioneers in family systems theory realized that schizophrenia was a family as well as an individual diagnosis, and they focused on the power imbalances that were going on in the family.

It is ironic that family systems theory, which widened the horizons of mental illness to include the family system and the central role of power imbalances, would make it difficult for practitioners to see beyond the family to the societal system. Not only was the social system out of sight, but the emotional, physical, and sexual abuse that resulted from extreme power imbalances also remained hidden. Why was it that pioneers in family systems theory could put themselves in the shoes of a person diagnosed as schizophrenic and imagine his or her experience of being overpowered within a family system, and not be able to put themselves in the shoes of a child being sexually abused, or a spouse who had been battered? Why could they not look beyond the family, and see the ways in which people were often caught in power struggles within societal systems? Perhaps it was too painful for systems theorists to continue to identify with the powerlessness experienced within family systems. Perhaps there was a greater need to affirm one's self-determination within the arena of the family and to affirm that the family could remain untouched by power imbalances in the culture.[3]

A circular understanding of power dynamics is broken when we acknowledge experiences of being overpowered. When we appreciate how easily power imbalances occur and the dangers we experience in the midst of power struggles, then we can also understand the grace of empowering relationships where there is a flow of energy, a give and take in which our worth is valued and not threatened. Carter Heyward describes the gospel story of the hemorrhaging woman as an instance of an empowering relationship:

And the woman who touched Jesus' garments "felt in her body that she was healed of her disease. And Jesus, perceiving in himself that power had gone forth from him, turned about in the crowd (Mark 5:29-30 [RSV])." A flow of power, a reciprocal situation, in which both persons are affected by what is happening between them. . . . The power that goes forth from Jesus, the power released by the woman's reaching and touching in faith, is power quite unlike the principalities and powers within/between/among us that seek control and domination over our own lives and the lives of others. (Heyward, 1984, 118)

Heyward reflects theologically on the process of empowerment:

We touch this strength, our power, who we are in the world, when we are most fully in touch with one another and with the world. There is no doubt in my mind that, in doing so, we are participants in ongoing incarnation, bringing god to life in the world. For god is nothing other than the eternally creative source of our relational power, our common strength, a god whose movement is to empower, bringing us into our own together. (Heyward, 1984, 124)

Empowering relationships incarnate fullness of being among us and within us. Poling (1991, 24) notes that "Within a process-relational view of reality, power in its ideal form is virtually synonymous with life itself." Such power is always within relationships where everyone is interconnected in a relational web that allows for both self-assertion and mutual recognition of one another's humanity.[4] This is not to say that empowering relationships can only exist among equals. In the necessarily hierarchical relationship that exists between a parent and child, empowering moments occur when both can claim their rights and needs as parents and children, and when both experience a sense of effectiveness and fulfillment. When Winnicott referred to the reciprocity of parent-child relationships, he meant that there needs to be an acknowledgment of parental needs as well as children's needs, with some give and take. If the process of reciprocity can occur, both parents and children will experience a sense of empowerment as they move through developmental transitions.

Similarly, a minister and parishioner will experience empowerment when both can act in effective ways, and when the needs and rights of both are recognized. For example, a minister informed of a parishioner's hospitalization can consider both her needs and the parishioner's needs. She may easily see her parishioner's need for a hospital visit but may ignore her own needs as she tries to fit a hospital visit into a long, busy day. She may lose sight of the relational web in which she lives, by acting as if her becoming worn out will not affect those with whom she is in relationship.

When power is seen as the energy of the relational web itself, then power can be understood as the ability to sustain internal relationships and increase the power of the relational web as a whole. (Poling, 1991, 25)

When we experience an empowering relationship and the enlivening flow of energy that moves back and forth, it is hard to understand why we so easily become caught in power struggles where it feels like someone has to win or lose. Guggenbuhl-Craig, writing of power struggles in therapeutic relationships, describes them as an evil from which we shall not be delivered, with which we must learn to deal. We can elaborate our understanding of power imbalances in pastoral care and counseling by exploring the forms it often takes: being domineering/feeling inadequate, being the expert/feeling overwhelmed by a lack of expertise, and becoming the aggressor/victim.

POWER IMBALANCES IN PASTORAL CARE AND COUNSELING

Perhaps the most common power imbalance experienced by clergy is the feeling of inadequacy. For example, the minister who feels *inadequate* when meeting with a family who has lost someone through death may become *domineering* as a way of coping with such feelings. She or he may take charge of the situation, quickly making decisions about what needs to be done or said. If this care giver is aware of feeling inadequate and wanting to take charge, then he or she is more likely to give family members room to approach this death in whatever ways they can. In this process, the care giver's professional responsibility is to *enable* those who mourn to face this death.

Related to the experience of feeling inadequate is the experience of feeling *overwhelmed by a lack of expertise*. This may be especially true in a time when, in many cultural communities, the public role of clergy is diminished and when pastoral care can seem so ill-defined when compared with a specialty like pastoral counseling. I often liken pastoral care to the role of midwife. The pastor is a supportive presence with individuals, couples, families, and communities in the midst of crises and transitions. The pastor monitors all dimensions of the movement through crisis or transition—spiritual, emotional, physical—as well as all the internested systems involved in the crisis or transition: intrapsychic, interpersonal, familial, communal, and cultural. She or he can recognize when people are stuck and when intervention is needed. When short-term interventions are not adequate, then he or she makes referrals. The pastoral care giver is always part of care-giving teams: the parish care-giving network, community resources, and denominational resources.

This metaphor of pastoral care giver as midwife highlights the likelihood of pastoral care givers feeling inadequate because they are not experts at making particular interventions in the way that a pastoral counselor trained in marriage and family therapy may be. When our sense of "not knowing" overwhelms us, then we may end up neglecting those we care for, and/or neglecting ourselves. I remember what a revelation it was to do a verbatim of a conversation with a parishioner in the hospital. I had been her pastoral care giver for several years and was doing a verbatim during a summer-long unit of supervised pastoral education in my own congregation. As my supervisor and I discussed the verbatim, I became vividly aware of how long I had been feeling critical of myself and this parishioner for what seemed like the lack of purpose in my pastoral ministry with her. The verbatim also made me aware of the purpose which was there but I discounted. My experience highlights how my seeming lack of expertise could result in neglecting my parishioner in that I might see her less often because of my frustration.[5]

The dangers of identifying too much with the role of *expert* are probably more a liability for specialists like pastoral counselors who develop particular areas of expertise. The liabilities of expertise are that we may use our knowledge to have power over others as a way of keeping them in a one-down position. When expertise becomes a means of having power over another, then both the expert and the recipient of this expertise lose their subjectivity and become objects.[6] When another becomes an object, we lose sight of his or her fullness of being.[7] He or she becomes categorized and reduced to representing something.[8] Guggenbuhl-Craig (1971) uses an archetypal perspective to describe how the internal archetype of healer-patient can become split, with the care giver becoming the expert at healing and the care receiver becoming the helpless patient who has no internal expertise at healing. In this process, healers become identified with their role of being a care giver, and this role is inflated so that it overpowers other aspects of the care giver's self, such as their own pain. When we exchange the word *healing* with terms like attunement and empathy, we can appreciate how much we come to expect the care giver to be an expert at attunement and empathy. In a culture in which attunement may be greatly lacking in many relational contexts (in the community, in work relationships, and in the corporate world) there may be a demand for "perfect attunement" in dyadic healing and nurturing relationships. The parent, the minister, the counselor, or the teacher is expected to be an expert at attunement and empathy. This is a variation of what Guggenbuhl-Craig (1971) calls the split-archetype of doctor-patient. The overvaluing of the care giver's expertise and devaluing of the care receiver's expertise create a power imbalance which can become abusive of both care giver and care receiver (noting that the care receiver is more at risk of being abused).

Guggenbuhl-Craig (1971) comments on the shadow side of the power imbalance that identifies one person as the healer and the other person as the patient. As healers we may become aggressive in our interventions, particularly when we identify ourselves as the expert. The potential for violence lurks in the shadow: "One welfare worker, for instance, dreamed that while driving his car he had run over a person on whom, in waking life, he had imposed certain things" (Guggenbuhl-Craig, 1971, 8). The shadow side of expertise can cast the expert in the role of the *aggressor*. The shadow side of being the patient can cast the one seeking care in the role of *victim*. At its most extreme, this shadow experience of being the patient can evoke images of pain being inflicted aggressively by the one giving care. I recall having an unpleasant dental procedure done, one which involved the dentist burning away a piece of my gum. His comment, "Smells like a barbecue in here," alluded to his shadow experience of being the aggressor and inflicting pain. My silent acceptance of his remark involved my identification with the shadow experience of being a victim. Had I immediately protested, I would have refused to be victimized. What hindered me is what hinders many people in similar situations: I was taken aback and I was in a one-down position physically. Lebacqz (1985) comments that we have failed to take into account the extent of the power imbalance between the professional and the client. My lack of protest was due to both intrapsychic inhibitions and the interpersonal ways the power imbalance inhibited me.

In this instance, however, the onus was not on me to take action. The onus is on the professional to monitor what Guggenbuhl-Craig calls the shadow side of being cast in the role of expert. So, for example, my dentist needed to monitor the images that were floating through his consciousness, not to censor them, but in order to keep them from slipping out, as the image of a human barbecue slipped out in his comment.

Under stress we may find the shadow side of the split archetype of expert/patient more present. Images of aggressor and victim may predominate. We may feel a compulsion to act these out. Given our particular histories, and given the sexually violent culture we are all a part of in North America, we may act out the images of aggressor and victim sexually. For example, a woman recounted how as a client she was negotiating an affordable fee with a pastoral counselor, a diplomate in the American Association of Pastoral Counselors. As part of this discussion, he asked her how "good she was in bed." She was taken aback and ignored his remark, bracketing it as not having anything to do with what they were talking about. In this instance, the expert became the aggressor, using sex as a way of overpowering the client. While his remark could have arisen out of a personal context of overwhelming stress, more likely it is part of an ongoing pattern of aggression toward female clients. Guggenbuhl-Craig (1971) names the harm done by acting upon such aggression as evil. Instead of offering help, we use our power as care givers to hurt and destroy. John Updike's portrait of a minister who is a sexual offender vividly depicts the destruction that results.

It is difficult when talking about the shadow side of being the expert/patient to understand the relationship between power imbalances that occur momentarily when we feel overwhelmed or inadequate, and those that involve wielding power to hurt or destroy. We may want to create two kinds of power imbalances: a "normal" power imbalance that occurs momentarily and which doesn't entail abusive words or actions, and malevolent power imbalances.[9] The value of

81

seeing violence as an extension of any power imbalance is that we can glimpse and monitor our own often unconscious potential for violence. As well, we may not so easily deny the violence we actually encounter in helping relationships.

As was seen most clearly in the sexual violence depicted in John Updike's novel *A Month of Sundays* and the racial violence depicted in Toni Morrison's *Beloved,* power imbalances become violent when there is disengagement and/or merger, and one loses sight of the other's humanity and worth. If one is able to imagine being in the shoes of the other, then one is less likely to act out in abusive ways. Imagining the experience of someone else is not easy or natural. It is a quality of relationship that comes about through a willingness to trust, risk, and invest time and energy in continual learning from one another.[10]

Once we are in these extreme power imbalances, we become more and more unable to step out of them. People who have established a pattern of responding to internal, interpersonal, and cultural conflict with violence will not be able to stop their violent behavior themselves. Similarly, the longer and more profoundly people are victimized by violence, the more they will be internally incapacitated to move out of a power struggle when given the chance to do so.[11] We see this not only in terms of intrapsychic, interpersonal, and family systems, but in international relationships. When nations begin to use violence as a way of resolving conflict, such violence can move to the extremes of terrorism, torture of political prisoners, and genocide. Intervention by the whole international community is the only way to break the cycle of violence, just as intervention by the whole community is the only way to break the cycle of violence in interpersonal and family systems.

THE CULTURAL DIMENSIONS OF POWER IMBALANCES

Having highlighted some of the intrapsychic and interpersonal dimensions of power struggles, I would like to highlight the cultural dimensions of power imbalances. Too often in the past, pastoral care and counseling have been oriented toward the individual, with seemingly no awareness of the extent to which power imbalances in the family, the community, and the culture are the context for the pain experienced by individuals.[12] When our ministry is so focused on the individual, the intrapsychic system, and goals of autonomy and self-realization, we join with the culture in focusing on individualism and privatism. Graham suggests that "Psychosystemic theory enables us to position the ministry of care more prominently among larger social and political interpretations of the pastoral situation, without losing the focus of the healing, sustaining, and guiding needed by individuals, groups, and families" (Graham, 1992, 12). In elaborating this psychosystemic perspective, Graham draws a series of internested systems with the psyche/soul as the innermost system, followed by the family, society, culture, nature, and God (Graham, 1992, 54). He then expands the traditional definition of pastoral ministry to include not only care of persons, but care of the world:

> Religious ministry is understood as the totality of strategic activities engaged in by the religious community and its individual members to increase the love of self, God and neighbor, and to promote a just social order and a livable environment. (Graham, 1992, 43)

What a psychosystemic perspective brings into focus are the power imbalances in the culture, and the "massive network of oppression and violence at the macrocosmic level" (Graham, 1992, 17):

> Whether we are aware of it or not, these systems organize our psyches and our behaviors into patterns of domination and subordination. (Graham, 1992, 17)

When pastoral care givers and counselors are not aware of power imbalances in the social order, then our ministry can actually be an attempt to make people more adaptive to the injustices they live with on a daily basis. It is critical that we be aware of the effects of power imbalances within the culture and not just in intrapsychic, familial, and interpersonal relationships.

I have already alluded to these power imbalances in the culture by describing the power gap that exists between professionals and clients. This power gap, along with the power afforded by expertise, makes it more likely that the technical language of the expert will be identified with "reality." Other discourses (the narrative account which the client uses, for example) may be discounted as irrelevant or even "inaccurate." The highly technical language of our areas of expertise may work against a recognition of the diversity of discourses on pain and healing, especially when expertise is overvalued and one's professional identity is often reduced to the knowledge one has.[13] For example, in 1993 there was an outbreak of a mysterious illness in the southwestern United States. Eventually, scientists traced its origins to rat droppings. In a radio program on how to take precautions, a health officer told people to avoid inhaling dust particles from these droppings, and a tribal medicine person spoke of how to cleanse the house spiritually. The contrast in their discourses was startling. I was aware of my own bias. I heard the health officer's words as "truth" and the spiritual healer's words as "superstition." It was difficult to hold both discourses as true.

Realizing that any definition of reality is socially constructed, and that there are many ways of defining reality may help us become more aware of the classism, racism, sexism, and homophobia enshrined in many constructions of reality. For example, Fernando (1989, 74-83) in a text on race and culture in psychiatry, reviews British research findings that demonstrate the ways in which the diagnosis of schizophrenia has been shaped by social problems, particularly problems concerning immigrant populations. This "raises questions, not just of diagnostic methodology, but also of the *social function* of this diagnosis within society" (Fernando, 1989, 96). Similarly, the diagnosis of depression among those marginalized by race may simply focus on the intrapsychic consequences of racism without looking at the social context. Fernando (1989, 44-49) also highlights the extent to which popular stereotypes,[14] European ideologies, assumptions, and social and political forces are as much part of making diagnoses and treatment plans as clinical and empirical observations. He illustrates this by describing the extent to which the powerful image of the dangerous Black male shapes diagnosis and treatment.

The same critiques that Fernando makes of the psychiatric literature can be applied to pastoral theological literature as a way of highlighting the limitations of how this discipline has "named reality." One critique is that racist ideology is often "disguised as views about culture" when race is equated with culture (Fernando, 1989, 52). In research and clinical practice, what are usually designated as "cultural groups" are in fact groups differentiated by race only. When the focus is on cultural differences, then the effect that one's designated race may have within a social context is blurred. For example, Fernando describes a study that explores the finding that referral practices on the part of general practitioners were different for Asian patients as compared with indigenous English patients. Fernando comments:

> Questions about "communication of information," "cultural taboos against revealing certain symptoms" and "lack of knowledge about patients' way of life" were delineated as possible reasons for the relative failure by general practitioners to refer their Asian patients to hospital, while racial discrimination by professionals, racism within psychiatric service and similar factors were disregarded. (Fernando, 1989, 52-53)

The focus on cross-cultural differences, particularly when done by those in dominant positions of power, can be a way of blurring the effects of racism when racism is not considered part of the equation. In recent literature, there has been a focus on cross-cultural pastoral care and counseling.[15] When such cross-cultural studies equate culture with race and leave racism out of the discussion, then they are defining reality in a way that blurs oppressive power hierarchies. Further, the tendency for such blurring will be more likely in authors who have not experienced marginalization because of racism. We need studies of race and culture in pastoral care and counseling from diverse racial perspectives in which the power imbalances created by racism remain in focus.

Often it is easy, in retrospect, to see the degree to which our pictures of reality are distorted by our biases. An instance of this is the literature on menopause. Historically, a common theme in the literature on menopause is that the major dynamic of this transition is women's grief over the loss of their reproductive capacities. In a cross-cultural study of five different cultural groups in Israel, it was demonstrated that "to the researcher's great astonishment women across the five cultures unanimously welcomed menopause and the cessation of fertility, despite great differences in childbearing history, and despite differences in attitude toward the size of their families" (Datan, 1990, 126). It has also been widely believed that difficulties with menopause are linked with children leaving home and the so-called empty-nest syndrome. No empirical study has demonstrated this. Depressive symptoms during menopause do not appear to be linked to psycho-social factors thought to be peculiar to the transitions

85

of life concurrent with menopause (e.g., children leaving home), but are related to more general, chronic, and pre-existing stressors, such as marital dissatisfaction, financial difficulties, and limited social networks and support systems (Greene, 1990, 103-104).

The myths about menopause can be used to illustrate not simply how the literature on menopause has distorted women's experience, but also the consequences of such distortion. When women are portrayed as becoming depressed when their reproductive capacity is over and when their children leave home, then stereotypes of motherhood are reinforced.

This discussion of power imbalances in culture, in particular the power imbalance created by those who identify their social constructions of reality with "truth," resonates with a philosophical perspective called post-structuralism. While this perspective may initially seem overly complex and intellectual, I believe it has great relevance to formulating what I call a post-modern[16] pastoral theology.

POWER IMBALANCES AND POST-STRUCTURALISM

The ways in which language can be used to overpower have been explored through post-structuralist philosophy and its offshoots: for example, post-structuralist theology and literary criticism. While an overview of such a broad and complex literature is beyond the scope of this chapter, even a brief summary of this literature affords some intriguing reflections on the power imbalances in pastoral care and counseling.

A simple way to understand this complex literature is to highlight the assumptions of a structuralist perspective. A structuralist perspective assumes that there is a deep structure to language and to works of art and human behavior. This deep underlying structure organizes every aspect of what can be called the surface structure of language, art, and human behavior.[17] Using a structuralist perspective, the surface of a musical work, literary text, or life story can be analyzed until the underlying themes or motifs emerge. For example, I can look at what is happening both vertically (in each voice) and horizontally (in harmonic chords) in a Bach fugue. I may see that a musical sentence in the leading voice can be "reduced" to this essential movement: from *do* to *so* to *do*. Then I may see that the three sections of the fugue are based on the same movement. The first section centers around *do,* the second around *so,* and the final section around *do.* This can be understood as the deep structure of the fugue. With a structuralist perspective we can "take an X ray" of the surface structure and see embedded in it the deep structure.

With a structuralist perspective, one assumes that there is one or a limited number of methods for deriving the deep structure. Often this assumption is not even questioned, as though getting to the deep structure is like archaeology: as long as one is careful in uncovering and piecing together the fragments, one will be able to arrive at a clear outline of the deep structure. A related assumption is that the author of the musical work, novel, or even narrative has a clear intention about what she or he is trying to say. If we can only understand the author better, then we will understand her or his intention.

Traditional theologies can be described as structuralist in that God is understood as the Author of creation, and the ultimate essence, truth, and meaning of all that is. Ontotheologians endeavor to study God as the Being qua Being: the deep structure of the universe and of our lives. If we could only know God better, we would understand how our lives and the world are ordered. Similarly, in biblical studies there has been an assumption that a particular method could uncover the meaning of a biblical text. Various methods of interpretation are put into a hierarchy, with some interpretative methods affording a "truer" way of getting at the meaning of the text.[18] Traditional scientific methods have been based on a structuralist stance, with the assumption that with enough scientific experiments, the whole blueprint and underlying order of matter could be discovered.

When we pay attention to the power imbalances created by a structuralist approach, we can see that the assumption that there is only one or only several methods for discovering (and not creating) truth means that those who are experts at these methods are given the power to name what is "true," since truth is identified with the deep structure. If there is an assumption that the deep structure is true in all places and at all times, then the "truth" is assumed to be transhistorical and transuniversal. Such "transhistorical and universal truths" become idolatrous, in that they become equated with some divine ordering of the world. Such "truths" may be not only irrelevant in many contexts, but may also be oppressive.

Our present era has been described as post-structuralist in that we can no longer maintain a deep confidence that science, objectivity, and technological competence themselves can serve as an orienting framework providing meaning and understanding. (Mitchell, 1993, 18)

Our era has also been called post-positivistic because we no longer have positivistic assumptions that one true method (for example, the scientific method) will uncover "truth," with progress understood as the accumulation of more and more "truth."

With a post-structuralistic perspective one becomes more aware of the potential totalitarianism of a structuralist worldview.[19] The paradox is that such a structuralist worldview, with its blueprint of a supremely ordered universe, would seem to be empowering and not overpowering. For example, the belief that we are in a covenantal relationship with a God who is the Being of all being, first Cause, and Meaning of all meaning seems to be profoundly empowering. Such a relationship may be especially empowering in a context where we feel overpowered by "life's precariousness and contingency, the ways in which we dangle over seventy thousand fathoms" (Huston Smith, 1989, 45, echoing an image from Kierkegaard). The liability of envisioning an all-powerful God with whom we are aligned is our tendency to use such a faith to overpower others and to claim absolute truths.

The complexities of post-structuralism may seem to take us far beyond an understanding of how power imbalances occur in pastoral care and counseling. However, when we turn to the fictional character the Reverend Tom Marshfield in John Updike's *A Month of Sundays,* we become aware of what Guggenbuhl-Craig has called the evil which we in the helping professions face. While it may be easy to distance ourselves from a character like Marshfield and deny any similarities, we are challenged by Updike to see the ways in which the violence that goes on within Marshfield's relationships is symptomatic of the culture in which we all live. Power imbalances will become more extreme when we identify our understanding of reality as truth, and when unconscious needs and fears pull us toward disengagement and merger. This was chillingly illustrated in Updike's novel when Marshfield described his "mystical" experience of giving communion to women he was sexually abusing.

Flinn (1989, 129) suggests that the most empowering stance can be "what Plato called the *metaxu,* the in-between." John Caputo

(1987) calls such a stance "living in the flux." Such a stance would empower us by allowing us to name what has ultimate meaning for us, and at the same time would bring a hermeneutic of suspicion to the horizons of meaning we create out of the particularities of our experience.[20] Iris Murdoch's character Anne Clavidge is an example of someone endeavoring to live in the flux. She is engaged in a lively, sensitive relationship with the "as-if" God and is led beyond her own horizons—first the horizons of the convent and then the horizons of her charged relationships with the Count and Gertrude. Her faith is founded upon a sense of who Jesus is for her ("her nomadic, cosmic Christ, uniquely hers").

In Updike's character we see the relational consequences of a minister caught in an intense power struggle who uses a distorted faith system to reinforce his disengagement from and power over others. A post-structuralist perspective helps us understand how the ways we define reality can be used to justify violence and abuse. In Murdoch's character Anne Clavidge we see the relational consequences of her relationship with God. Her tolerance of ambiguity, her utter certainty of who Jesus is for her, and her sense of his continual presence with her lead her to reject the comforts of home within the convent and in Gertrude's circle of friends. In a time when we all long for theological "homes" where there is certainty and shelter from pure relativism,[21] Murdoch reminds us of the risks of creating such homes and the courage it takes to leave such homes. Taking such risks and having this courage (some of the qualities of living "in-between") greatly shape our pastoral care relationships. We will more likely be open to the energy generated within our relationships and more able to move beyond our own horizons and glimpse multiple horizons of meaning.

A specific consequence of living "in-between" is described by Brueggemann as he likens a postmodern interpretation of the Bible to therapeutic talk:

> First, therapeutic talk, when it is serious, does not concern large schematic settlements of one's life, but depends upon going beneath the visible structures of self to the little, specific details that hold hidden power over us. . . . And out of these little bitty pieces of memory may come the stuff of new self-discernment, and eventually, of new self. . . .

Second, the therapist does not have to see everything or know everything in advance. It is enough to surface and hold and honor the little pieces, to savor their potentially revelatory power. . . .

Third, it is the unguarded rumination, without focused or disciplined meaning, that may trigger an insight, a connection, an illumination that liberates and heals. Such therapeutic conversation is exceedingly difficult for those of us who are too sure, too settled, too established. (Brueggemann, 1993, 21)

Brueggemann's description of a therapeutic relationship does not make explicit the quality of relationship that is so important in pastoral care and counseling. I have noted the ways in which merged and disengaged dynamics when combined with power imbalances can result in abuse. An empathic relationship with its openness to and valuing of one another's worth involves both a sense of connection with and separation from the other. I will explore this quality of relationship by describing relational boundaries in pastoral care and counseling.

RELATIONAL BOUNDARIES IN PASTORAL CARE AND COUNSELING

DEFINING MERGER AND DISENGAGEMENT

In Iris Murdoch's novel *Nuns and Soldiers,* one of the characters, Gertrude, wants to keep her circle of friends close to her. She makes a deal with a friend, the Count, who is infatuated with her. She promises that he can always be her faithful attendant. When she tries to make her friend Anne Clavidge a part of this "family" Anne refuses. This angers Gertrude, and we glimpse the intense need that lies beneath her beneficence. Gertrude says that she can't do without her and that Anne is *her* nun. The "sheepfold" that Gertrude wants to create involves merger: a desire to absorb others within a family system she creates. The Count accepts the terms of agreement and Anne refuses.

The word *merge* has legal origins, where it means "to sink or extinguish (a lesser estate, title, or such) in one which is greater or superior" (*Oxford English Dictionary,* 355). From this legal usage comes its more general usage: "to cause [something] to be absorbed into something else, so as to lose its own character or identity" and "to sink and disappear, to be swallowed up and lost to view" (*Oxford English Dictionary,* 355).

Another word for merger is *fusion.* This word has its origins in the world of physics: heating something until it becomes fluid; blending together different things "as if by melting so as to form one whole" (*Oxford English Dictionary,* 623). A fused relationship, unlike a merged relationship, does not involve a power imbalance. In a merged relationship, one person is subsumed in another. The boundaries of the dominant person remain intact, and the boundaries of the subordinate person dissolve as he or she is swallowed up. An example of a merged relationship would be a parent-child relationship where the child is absorbed in the parent's world. In a fused relationship, both persons undergo a dissolution of boundaries. The example I opened with is a merged relationship because Gertrude wants to absorb others within her household. Since relational boundaries interact with power dynamics, a loss of boundaries often involves a power struggle, creating merged relationships.

Merger and fusion describe extremes. Our usual experiences of merger are not so extreme, and could be described as blurred boundaries or boundary encroachment. We may at times become over-involved emotionally with a parishioner or client. For example, instead of working with a family in crisis so that together we reflect on how they can cope during the next few days, we may find ourselves giving advice and taking over. It may be hard for us to leave at the end of a pastoral care visit because we feel as though the family members can't manage on their own. Sometimes I experience boundary encroachment physiologically. I may slump in my chair and feel worn out when sitting with people who are depressed. My own body mirrors their body and I lose a sense of my body as different from theirs. I remember being with someone who was in a manic episode. Her mood was contagious. I started to feel as agitated as she was. She talked with a sense of great urgency about somewhere she had to go immediately. She wanted me to drive her there. My agitation took the form of envisioning some sort of catastrophe. If we didn't go, something terrible might happen, and if we did go, something equally disastrous could occur, like a car accident.

In reflecting on merged or fused relationships in families, it is helpful to use the term *boundary* in a literal sense. For example, when are doors shut and when are they kept open? Is the bathroom door kept shut when a parent is having a bath? Are parents able to shut and lock the bedroom door, if that is what they need to do in order to have privacy for love-making? When teenagers insist on leaving their rooms in chaos, are parents able to shut the door and ignore the disorder? Do spouses open one another's mail? These are all questions concerning interpersonal boundaries and the extent to which relationships are merged or fused.

A disengaged relationship appears at first glance to be the opposite of merger. The dictionary definition of disengagement is intriguing: "to loosen from that which holds fast, adheres or entangles; to detach, liberate, free" (*Oxford English Dictionary*, 444). When *engagement*—intellectual, spiritual, emotional, physical—is likened to being bound, held fast, and entangled, then *disengagement* is liberating. As I use the term, disengagement describes a quality of relational boundaries having to do with being emotionally, intellectually, and spiritually distant and withdrawn to such an extent that one is experienced as being far away, even in outer space.[1]

We can again reflect on family relationships and the degree of disengagement by reflecting on boundaries. To what extent are the parents involved in their children's school work? If the extent of contact is the parent silently reading a report card each semester, then the parent is disengaged from the child. If, on the other hand, parents are so involved that they take over school projects, then the relationship becomes merged in these moments of taking over homework. In John Updike's novel *A Month of Sundays*, Reverend Marshfield describes his childhood home as disengaged. There seems to be little intimacy in his parents' marriage, and between him and his parents. As a toddler, his most immediate contact is with the furniture in the house.

Boundaries can also be used as a metaphor for what happens intrapsychically. Intrapsychic boundaries can be relatively thick and solid or thin and permeable, depending on whether one is in a disengaged or a merged stance:

> There are people who strike us as very solid and well organized; they keep everything in its place. They are well defended. They seem rigid, even armored; we sometimes speak of them as "thick-skinned." Such people, in my view, have very thick boundaries. At the other extreme are people who are especially sensitive, open or vulnerable. In their minds, things are relatively fluid; they experience thoughts and feelings—often many different feelings—at the same time. Such people have particularly thin boundaries. (Hartmann, 1991, 4)[2]

As was illustrated in John Updike's novel *A Month of Sundays*, there can be shifts from disengagement to merger. When the Reverend Tom Marshfield first meets Ms. Prynne, the manageress of his desert "retreat center," he pictures her as a snapping turtle and feels repulsed by her. Later in the novel, when someone writes a comment in his daily journal, he feels suddenly vulnerable. He imagines that Ms. Prynne is reading his journal, and starts to have intense needs for contact with her. These needs escalate to the point of panic, and he feels as though he is disintegrating and only she can put him back together. His longing for sexual union is actually for merger.

In any major crisis or transition we may experience fluctuations between disengagement and merger: between thick, rigid boundaries and thin, permeable boundaries. The most vivid example of this is what can happen in the aftermath of an overwhelming life-threatening event. People can often experience an alternation between re-experiencing the traumatic event through dreams and flashbacks and avoiding anything that is associated with the traumatization. Readers of Morrison's novel *Beloved* can hear this alternation between disengagement and merger in the way Sethe tries to shut out memories and then becomes flooded with them. One way she copes with traumatic memories is to cut herself off from everyone but her children and mother-in-law. In the process she numbs herself to the world around her; for example, she doesn't notice colors. When an old friend appears and she begins to remember the past in the comfort of his presence, she suddenly starts seeing colors again. She wonders whether she became color-blind after seeing the redness of her murdered daughter's blood and the pink of the tombstone against her back, as she submitted to sex in order to get the engraver to put "beloved" on the stone. As we can see in Morrison's character Sethe, the disengagement that was once a way to cope with traumatization can become established as a personality change, described by Titchener (1986, 18) as post-traumatic decline "which results in the removal of the person from meaningful participation in family, society, work, and all forms of gratification."

The pull toward disengagement, with its thickening and stiffening of boundaries, can also be described in terms of one's belief system. When a transition or crisis becomes overwhelming, people may cope by developing a belief system that creates a firm, solid structure in the midst of overwhelming events. For example, when Iris Murdoch's character Anne Clavidge becomes involved in many sexual relationships in university, she begins to long for some return to "innocence" and "simplicity." She not only converts to Catholicism, but enters religious life as a way to step out of the "carnival" and "maelstrom" of sex. She does not ultimately cling to the highly structured religious life and faith system in which she has immersed herself. She is able to recognize when it is time for her to move out of this "home."

In Updike's character the Reverend Tom Marshfield, we see a similar movement toward a more structured religious system in the process of leaving home. As a young man Marshfield disparages the theological liberalism of his father and father-in-law and turns toward Barth, whose voice seems stronger and surer than his father's. His neo-orthodoxy is not ultimately part of an evolving relationship with God (as religious life is for Anne Clavidge) but becomes an empty theology, a way of reacting to the power struggles he experiences with men around him.

The paradox of relational boundaries is that one can be part of mergers and be disengaged at the same time. This is what happens in racism, when people are disengaged from those identified as racially different. At the heart of such disengagement is a refusal to see the humanity of those who are different. Combined with disengagement is a projection of racial stereotypes. In the process of projection there is a demand that those who are different conform to the stereotypes. In Morrison's novel *Beloved* the slave owner called Schoolteacher demands that his slaves step into the roles he has created for them in his intrapsychic world: the roles of being part animal. The more urgently he demands that they conform to this stereotype, the more violent he becomes.

GENDER DIFFERENCES AND
THE PULL TOWARD DISENGAGEMENT OR MERGER

There may be a tendency for men to move interpersonally toward disengagement during times of stress, since the formation of male gender identity coincides with separation from their maternal care giver. What it means to be male and female is formed as toddlers move through the intricate processes of separating from their primary caretakers, learning language, becoming aware of sexual differences, and identifying more with their fathers or mothers, depending on their sex. Psychoanalytic theorists (Chodorow, 1978; Stoller, 1975) have speculated that when women are the primary caretakers during infancy and into the second year of development, boys will need to separate more radically in order to establish their gender identity, while girls will not need such a radical separation because they share the same gender identity as their primary caretaker (Chodorow, 1978). The radical separation negotiated between boys and their mothers has been described as the first step on their heroic, stoic journeys so exemplified in Euro-American folklore, mythology, and population culture, and indeed in developmental theories that identify independence, individuation, and separation with maturity and health.[3]

Some of Raymond Carver's short stories describe instances of disengagement that are typical of some Euro-American men in our culture. For example, in "So much water so close to home" (Carver, 1988), a woman named Claire struggles with her reactions to her husband's detachment, made painfully clear to her in the way he and his buddies respond to finding a dead woman floating in a stream. Stuart and his friends are described as "decent men, family men, responsible at their jobs" who "play poker, bowl and fish together" (Carver, 1988, 161). One Memorial Day weekend, they hike to a river to camp and do some fishing. They find the body of a nude woman floating in the river. The men aren't sure what to do. One of the men wants to go back to their cars right away. The others want to stay. They set up camp. After drinking whiskey around the campfire, they decide they better do something so that the woman's body doesn't float away. One of the men wades out into the cold river, takes hold of the "girl's" hand and pulls the body, which is floating face down, toward the shore. They use a nylon rope to secure her, one end tied around her wrist, the other around the roots of a tree.

The narrator Claire goes on to describe how the men fished throughout the weekend, cooked, ate, drank whiskey—washing their dishes in the river, "a few yards from where the body lay in the water" (Carver, 1988, 162). Around the campfire they "told coarse stories and spoke of vulgar or dishonest escapades out of their past, and no one mentioned the woman until Gordon Johnson, who'd forgotten for a moment, commented on the firmness of the trout they'd caught, and the terrible coldness of the river water" (Carver, 1988, 162).

The story describes Claire's anger and horror at her husband's actions and her struggle to understand his detachment. She is immersed in vivid images of the men and the dead woman and imagines herself as the dead woman: "I float toward the pond, eyes open, face down, staring at the rocks and the moss on the creek bottom," and then she thinks "nothing will be any different. We will go on and on and on and on. We will go on even now as if nothing had happened" (Carver, 1988, 166).

The story highlights how Claire's response is opposite to her husband's. His cool detachment contrasts with her sense of being immersed in images of the dead woman. Her emotional involvement is such that she drives 117 miles to attend the woman's funeral. In the closing section of the story, Claire continues to be immersed in the crisis of the woman's brutal death, while Stuart remains detached. She tells her husband that she is afraid. Her husband wants to help, saying that that is what husbands are for. Claire can't explain her fears. Stuart offers to take care of her by "playing doctor" and begins unbuttoning her blouse.

As is so poignantly depicted in Carver's story, Claire moves toward merger with the dead woman while Stuart is disengaged. The intrapsychic alternation between avoidance and intrusion of images associated with the dead woman is transposed to an interpersonal level, with Claire losing herself in the images of the dead woman and her husband remaining disengaged. The violence induced by such dynamics is evident in the physical violence that erupts between Claire and her husband at the end of the story. She slaps him and he lifts her up and throws her down after she rebukes his sexual overtures. He later breaks the lock on her bedroom door, just to show her that he can.

Claire's confusing feelings and images as she identifies with the dead woman are the wellsprings of an impassioned cry for justice. Her identification with the dead woman makes this woman a real human being, like herself. When no one is able to identify with those who are violated, the stage is set for violence. The liability for women like Claire is that they merge so completely with the other that they lose any sense of who they are. It may be harder for women—and indeed any person who is marginalized within a culture—to develop and maintain a firm sense of who they are. As Jean Baker Miller (1976) has described, those who are marginalized may develop a high degree of attunement to those in a dominant position while having difficulty being attuned to themselves. Developmental theorists who explore gender differences have suggested that the value system engendered in girls may incline them to value relationships over independence, and connection over separation (Gilligan, 1982). Women may have more difficulty moving appropriately into separation and letting go. They may be more inclined to maintain connection and hold on. As Marge Piercy writes in a poem entitled "To Have Without Holding," "Learning to love differently is hard, love with the hands wide open . . ." She describes how women usually hold on, "It hurts to thwart the reflexes / of grab, of clutch, to love and let / go again and again" (Piercy, 1980, 40).

During critical times of transition, men and women may handle stress by merging with their roles—as wife or husband, mother or father—and may find it easier initially to "lose" the aspects of themselves which don't fit smoothly into these roles. Margaret Atwood (1969) described this process in her novel, *The Edible Woman.* The protagonist, Marian, becomes engaged to be married and feels immediately that she is caught in the fantasy her fiancé and society have of what a wife is. She experiences this "being caught" as being consumed, and she begins to identify with the food that she is eating. This happens as she is watching her fiancé carve a steak. Marian pictures a diagram from one of her cookbooks: a cow with dotted lines on it, showing various cuts of meat. Suddenly she loses her appetite. As the days pass, she finds that she is unable to eat meat or chicken, and she fears that more and more "devourable" foods will become "non-devourable" (Atwood, 1969, 169).

She watches a friend, Clara, "disappearing" in the chaos of raising young children. Clara's husband explains to Marian what happens to a woman after marriage. Her

> core gets invaded. . . . The centre of her personality, the thing she's built up; her image of herself, if you like. . . . She allows her core to get taken over by the husband. When the kids come, she wakes up one morning and discovers she doesn't have anything left inside, she's hollow, she doesn't know who she is anymore; her core has been destroyed. (Atwood, 1969, 261)

As the sense of merger and being absorbed in her future husband's world and society's images of marriage increase, Marian identifies more and more with the food that she is eating. Every time she imagines that the food she is eating is alive, she is unable to eat it anymore. A soft-boiled egg looks up at her "with its one significant and accusing yellow eye" (Atwood, 1969, 178). She imagines a carrot making a sound, "A scream too low for us to hear" (Atwood, 1969, 197). Canned rice pudding becomes small cocoons with miniature living creatures inside. Cake tastes spongy and cellular, "bursting of thousands of tiny lungs" (Atwood, 1969, 230). Finally, there is almost nothing left that she can eat.

A turning point comes when she flees from a party at her fiancé's apartment. Her flight becomes an escape from her engagement and all that it represents. She returns home, gathers flour, eggs, butter, and vanilla and assembles a cake in the shape of a woman. She carefully "dresses" the cake-woman with frosting, and then attacks it with gusto.

In depicting Marian's internal process of picturing the food she eats as alive and losing her appetite, Atwood describes how images and physical sensation fuse to create a symbolic language depicting a woman's experience, when those around her cannot help her make sense of her feelings of merger. In Marian's circle of friends and associates, no one describes becoming engaged as being consumed. When Marian alludes to what is happening in a conversation with a friend, the friend describes this as pre-marriage nervousness typical of all brides. In the end, Marian trusts the truth of her internal symbolic language and acts upon it.

In *The Edible Woman,* we see how Marian overidentifies with her new role as fiancée and feels submerged. In the novel *As for Me and My House,* Ross Sinclair describes how a minister and his wife use their role as clergy to avoid intimacy. When they leave their prairie town for a summer vacation, they cannot step out of their roles. Mrs. Bentley is aware of how stiff and awkward they are with other people. Her husband sounds "like a priggish young evangelist," and she hears herself sounding sanctimonious (Ross, 1941, 93).

By focusing on the extremes of disengagement and merger, I have illustrated the extent to which we can alternate between one extreme and the other, and how gender may play a role in this. The dictionary definition of disengagement—"to loosen from that which holds fast, adheres or entangles; to detach, liberate, free" (*Oxford English Diction-*

ary, 444)—describes a reaction to merger. We can understand empathic moments in relationships as moments in which there is a delicate balance between experiencing what is going on deep within us, within the other and between us.

THE DELICATE BALANCE OF EMPATHIC MOMENTS

> We enter this evening as we enter a quartet
> Listening again for its particular note
> The interval where all seems possible,
> Order within time when action is suspended
> And we are pure in heart, perfect in will.
> We enter the evening whole and well-defended
> But at the quick of self, intense detachment
> That is a point of burning far from passion—
> And this, we know, is what we always meant
> And even love must learn it in some fashion,
> To move like formal music through the heart,
> To be achieved like some high difficult art.
> (May Sarton, "Evening Music," 1978, 49)

In her love poem, May Sarton describes the need to be separate in the midst of love: "at the quick of self, intense detachment, That is a point of burning far from passion—." The delicate balance between attachment and detachment describes an empathic moment.

Judith Jordan describes empathy as a three-part process. In order to be empathic, one must first have a basic motivation and capacity for human relatedness, such that one is paying attention to glimpses of what is going on inside of oneself and inside of the other. These glimpses may draw one toward the other. Empathy involves a capacity to look within (introspection) and to imagine what it would be like for the other to look within and become aware of what was happening to him or her (vicarious introspection).[4]

The second part of this movement is a surrender to affective and cognitive arousal in oneself. One is able to stand within the other's shoes and imagine what it is like for him or her. Jordan calls this being affectively connected, but the connection may be multidimensional, involving intellectual, spiritual, and artistic dimensions of connection. Concurrent to this standing within the other's shoes is one's awareness of one's separateness. In her love poem, Sarton describes this as an intense detachment at the quick of self, involving a burning far from passion. Empathy involves some boundary flexibility, such that one stands with the other but is still able to maintain a sense of oneself as different from the other. As well, empathy holds in tension the healthy polarities of (1) valuing subjective and objective experience and knowledge; (2) both understanding (going deeper into) and explaining (gaining an overview); (3) drawing upon knowledge gained from being connected with and separated from the other; and (4) both doubting and believing (Schlauch, 1990, 8). We can note that when we move toward one pole, we risk becoming disengaged (becoming objective, separated from the other, doubting and explaining) or merged (too subjective, understanding, connected, and believing).[5] In the third movement, the resolution period, one regains a sense of separate self, with an understanding of what has happened in the empathic experience.

Describing empathy in three parts implies a rather mechanical, step-by-step process. Often empathy is experienced as a moment in which we simultaneously feel intensely present and able to transcend what is happening. James Joyce has likened such moments to epiphanies; he describes such an epiphany in his short story, "The Dead." The story is about Gabriel, a middle-aged man who takes his wife to an annual Christmas party held by his aunts. Gabriel yearns for a sense of connection with his wife, his aunts, and those he encounters, yet continually feels isolated. The story proceeds through a series of pained interactions, where Gabriel is left feeling awkward, confused and shut out. At the end of the story, when he is getting undressed and ready for bed, Gabriel catches a glimpse of himself in the mirror and the glimpse widens into a lyrical translucent moment in which he suddenly can understand and appreciate his wife's sorrow and loss, and his own as well. The snow falling gently on Dublin, which has reminded him of his own disengagement, now becomes an image of the painful loneliness of all those in Ireland—an image that connects him with others instead of estranging him.

May Sarton (1978, 72) uses the image of doctor as angel to describe God's immanence in the healing moments of therapy and the mystery of the healing: "angels do not operate / By any means we can define." A crucial component of the healing moment is the doctor's paradoxical presence of standing with and standing apart: "the impersonal wing / Does shelter, provides a place, a climate / Where the soul can meet itself at last" (Sarton, 1978, 71). This presence creates the healing moment that provides shelter where we can experience ourselves "as a complex whole." Toni Morrison depicts this process in her novel *Beloved*. Paul is described as a blessed person in whose presence women can weep and feel their own sorrows. In the circle of his arms, Sethe remembers the night before she ran away and weeps for herself, her lost husband, and her children. Paul can resonate with her pain and stand with her without becoming overwhelmed. In the same way, he can feel the pain of the murdered child washing over him without drowning in its longing and rage.

EMPATHY AND PASTORAL CARE AND COUNSELING

Empathy has been described as the essence of pastoral psychotherapy (Schlauch, 1990). I understand empathic moments as moments when we see more fully who we are, who the other is, and what is happening between us. These are moments of recognition.[6] Given that we are so often pulled consciously and unconsciously toward merger or disengagement with their respective loss and entrenchment of boundaries, we often are not able to get our bearings in terms of seeing what is going on within us and the other and between us. An empathic moment is like a momentary lifting of the fog.

While this may seem like an unduly pessimistic view of relationships, I want to emphasize the role of the unconscious and the ways in which we often overvalue our insights. I also want to imply that empathy is not a mechanical process that we can learn from reading a book or following an instructional manual. Judith Jordan's description of the three movements of empathy may seem like the diagrams painted on the floors of Arthur Murray dance studios. Putting one's feet in the right place may mimic in slow motion the movements of dancing, but is not the way one is going to learn to feel the music within oneself, within one's partner, and in the push and pull of body contact between the two dancers. Sometimes we try to teach empathy by describing active listening and emphasizing communication skills. These strategies may not bring about empathic moments. Empathic moments come about when we have experienced profound relatedness in which our experiences resonate with the experiences of others in ways that allow us to see and feel the depths of these experiences without being overwhelmed.

Such moments shape us as pastoral care givers and counselors, whether they come in early childhood, in intimate relationships, in experiences with our children, in our own therapy, or within the community of faith. Remembering empathic moments can be a way to get our bearings in pastoral care and counseling relationships.

Another way to get our bearings is by deepening our awareness of how we react to stress. Stressful experiences in pastoral care and counseling can often pull us toward the kind of relational boundaries that were present in formative experiences. For example, I was raised in a family that valued maintaining emotional distance when stress was high, as if feelings created overwhelming chaos and the best way to handle any situation was to maintain a cool and calm appearance. My typical response to stress as an adult is to emotionally disengage and keep my feelings "frozen" until the "storm" is over. Another pastoral care giver may react to stress by experiencing an overflow of feelings—sadness, anger, and fear—and may worry that her feelings will make it too difficult for her to conduct a funeral service or chair a turbulent congregational meeting. She may find herself getting so caught up in pastoral crises that it's hard for her to let go of them.

While we can't learn how to be part of empathic relationships from reading about empathy, we can begin to reflect upon our own experiences, particularly our formative and transformative experiences, and the power dynamics and relational boundaries that were part of them. In the next chapter, I will consider how these dynamics can interact to create life-giving and potentially abusive relationships, and how we experience God in the midst of these relationships.

CHAPTER SIX

THE INTERACTION OF POWER DYNAMICS AND RELATIONAL BOUNDARIES IN OUR RELATIONSHIP WITH GOD

E mpathy and empowerment work together to create life-giving dynamics in relationships.[1] The terms *empathy* and *empowerment* are almost interchangeable, in that one implies the other. For example, in gospel stories of healing, Jesus is attuned to the pain of those around him, and those who are healed experience this empathy and are empowered through faith. Jesus' profound presence with those in pain was liberating. Heyward (1984, 124) uses the words *relational power* and *common strength* to describe those relationships in which we are "most in touch with one another and with the world." In her description, empowering and empathic dynamics intertwine in the process of creation, incarnation, and redemption. William Blake alludes to the empathy of God, exemplified in Jesus' response to those around him:

> Can I see another's woe,
> And not be in sorrow too? . . .
> Can I see a falling tear,
> And not feel my sorrow's share? . . .
> And can he who smiles on all
> Hear the wren with sorrows small.
> Hear the small bird's grief and care,
> Hear the woes that infants bear,
> And not sit beside the nest,
> Pouring pity in their breast;
> And not sit the cradle near,
> Weeping tear on infant's tear . . .

When May Sarton implicitly describes empathy in her poem "Evening Music," she alludes to being empowered: "the interval where all seems possible." James Nelson calls empathy and empowerment a passion for connection: the divine eros.[2]

When I consider my own life experience, I can appreciate the extent to which life events in which empathy and empowerment intertwine can transform earlier formative experiences in which abusive or neglectful dynamics predominated. The most vivid example of this was the experience I described at the outset of this book: my experience of being on a silent retreat and returning to the formative event of being sexually assaulted. Looking back, I can see now that I started to become a mother to myself in the process of caring so intensely for my infant son. My earlier experience of violence and neglect had left me disengaged from everything to do with the assault and its aftermath, except the feelings of intense anxiety that would flood me. The only way I could care for myself as an adolescent was to remain hyperalert to the warning signs of impending violence. Now as a woman who had experienced the goodness of my body in the process of childbirth and nursing, I was ready to remember. My feelings toward my infant were the embers that slowly kindled an empathy for myself. My spiritual director's presence and the tangible signs of God's presence in the symbols of communion and in the places of worship that surrounded me became the container for an emerging sense of empathy toward myself, and with it a sense of empowerment. As the prayer I wrote illustrates, this empathy and empowerment were rooted in the revelation that God was with me in my childhood experience. God's presence meant that this experience could not ultimately overpower me.

I have found it helpful, in reflecting on my own life, to name those life experiences in which disengagement, merger, and overpowering dynamics predominated as experiences that threatened to deform me. Experiences where empathy and empowerment predominated have been transformative events which have healed old wounds and opened up the potential for wholeness and fullness of being.[3]

Empathy and empowerment are creative, redeeming, and sustaining dynamics in relationships. Describing our relationship with God in terms of power dynamics and relational boundaries is a helpful way to evaluate our images of God—our personal images of God and those of our communities of faith and our religious traditions. Our images of God are formed in part through significant relationships, especially those relationships which are critical in formative and transformative events. Psychologists of religion have used an object relations model of personality to understand individuals' images of God. This model developed out of a Freudian model of personality. Whereas Freud saw the personality as energized by two drives or instincts (aggression and libido), object relations theorists saw these drives as occurring within relationships, like the relationship between the internal figures of father and self. In describing the formation of personality, object relations theorists emphasize the way we slowly form internal images of significant people: images of mother, father, siblings, and care takers, for example. In forming object representations, the child's raw data comes not from the external object (the mother or father) per se, but from sensations arising from various sources. These sensations form a multitude of impressions: a whole range, for example, of mother images (Sandler and Rosenblatt, 1962, 132-133). In this way, raw sensory data becomes transformed by the child into representations which create meaning:

> Representations are organized compilations of past experiences, relatively enduring impressions, constellations of perceptions and images, which the child culls from his [or her] various experiences and which in turn provide for the child a kind of cognitive map, a subjective landscape within which he [or she] can locate and evoke the cast of characters and events within the drama of his [or her] experience. (Greenberg and Mitchell, 1983, 373)

An object representation is an *unconscious* psychic organization which is the source of the conscious symbols, images, fantasies, thoughts, feelings, or actions (Beres and Joseph, 1970).

We can appreciate how important the formation of internal representations is in early childhood. The more the toddler can evoke the memory of her primary caretakers, the more she can tolerate separation from them. An important aid to separation is the availability of transitional objects. This is what Winnicott (1960) called those objects (teddy bears, blankets, and such) to which children become attached. Transitional objects "stand in for" the comforting presence of a caretaker. Such objects are also transitional representations in that "[they are] not actually taken to be the mother, and yet are also not fully an abstract symbolic representation of her. [They are] transitional in the movement from concrete representation to the achievement of a true symbol" (Eagle, 1984, 194). The sensuous qualities of the teddy bear or blanket (the smell, the feel of the satiny edge of a blanket) evoke the soothing a child receives from sensory contact with a caretaker.[4]

Two of the novels I reflected on earlier say something about early childhood experiences and allude to how these experiences affect relationships in adulthood. In John Updike's novel *A Month of Sundays,* Tom Marshfield describes his early childhood memories of being alone in a silent home and his fancy being engaged by the furniture. When he was a boy, furniture became more clearly connected with his father and the enjoyment he experienced watching his father's carpentry. Marshfield is conscious of the benevolent dynamics of these experiences, and the way in which they shaped his relationship with God as creator. The malevolent qualities of his early childhood experiences, which remain unconscious, were related to an intense desire to overpower and invade. These qualities could be connected with his mother, to whom he does not refer. When Marshfield is puttying a window, the smell and feel of wood and putty and the movement of bending his head close to the window remind him simultaneously of God the father and the genitals of a red-haired woman. In these associations, we see traces of object representations from early childhood. Images of his father and God as father are invoked. With these images come sexual imagery and a desire to possess a woman. While Marshfield is aware of the connections between father, God, and woodwork, he does not reflect on the origins of his sexual images and his desire for possession.

In *Beloved,* Toni Morrison describes what it is like when mothers are separated from their babies and how they experience intense yearning for physical contact followed by panic when this is not possible. Sethe was separated as a toddler from her own mother. She was haunted by a memory from early childhood: her mother showing her the brandmark on her skin so that Sethe would know who her mother was. Her being deprived of physical contact with her mother made it painful for her to be separated from her children, and fueled her determination to keep them with her even if it meant killing them.

The wailing anguish of the murdered child is ever-present, not only intrapsychically in Sethe, but in the haunting of the house.

When Stamp Paid, the elderly ex-slave who rescued Sethe, approaches the haunted house, he hears a cacophony of urgent voices and gradually he discerns the word "Mine." He realizes that this "pack of haunts" are "the people of broken necks, . . . and black girls who had lost their ribbons" (Morrison, 1987, 181). Morrison briefly immerses us in this wailing world of spirits. This is like being in the world of a preverbal child who is overwhelmed with need and separated from her mother. Such early childhood experiences of being separated from one's mother not only shaped Sethe but shaped whole generations of slaves and ex-slaves.

Psychologists of religion (Rizutto, 1979; Meissner, 1977, 1978, 1984, 1987; McDargh, 1983; Randour and Bondanza, 1987; Spero, 1992) have described how our images of God are formed in part from bits and pieces of internal representations of significant others. Updike's character Tom Marshfield illustrates this. He refers to the link between his childhood fascination with furniture and his sense of God as creator when he jokingly writes that he had no choice but to follow his father into the ministry—the furniture made him do it. The positive influence of sharing his father's hobby of carpentry shapes his images of God. The reader can also sense the ways in which the internal representations of an absent and seemingly powerful mother become a potent "god," that is, a powerful intrapsychic force that shapes his relationships. Marshfield engages in life and death battles with this "god." When he tries to break the faith of Frankie Harlow, the parishioner with whom he remains "ompotent," he is battling some inner demon which he projects onto her. The powerful unconscious representations associated with women take over his relationships, and are a much more real and immediate force in his life than the distant, remote images of the furniture-maker God of his espoused belief system.

Psychologists of religion have usually maintained a psychologistic stance by describing in wholly internal terms how God images are derived: "God representations themselves, according to this school [the prevailing psychologistic view] are attributed to psychic manufacture rather than any actual form of interchange between a human and a veridically existing divinity" (Spero, 1992, 15). A religionistic assumption is that God representations are not only internally derived, but also are externally derived from one's relationship with God. Spero proposes that there are two sources of God representations: interpersonal relationships (an anthropocentric source) and direct or indirect relationships with an objective God (a deocentric—some would say theocentric—source).[5] Spero (1992) develops a model of the formation of both anthropocentric and deocentric God representations that includes a divine object as part of the external reality. Sometimes none of the "cast of characters" (within the interpersonal and/or intrapsychic system) in a transformative event act in ways that are empathic and empowering. There is nothing life-giving among these intrapsychic and interpersonal relationships that can contribute to a life-giving anthropocentric God representation. In spite of this, the individual is able to apprehend a sense of God's empathic, empowering presence in the midst of an event where no person is mediating this presence.

In Toni Morrison's novel *Beloved,* Sethe's mother-in-law has this experience. There seemed to be nothing in her childhood or adult life that mediated a sense of God's presence. She described how her separation from her own mother when she was an infant and her later separation from her children gave her no memories of being held in a loving gaze that would instill a sense of her own self. She wonders whether her mother would have loved her, had her mother known her, and she feels a desolate emptiness within her. These moments of experiencing a sense of soul-less-ness are in sharp contrast to the moments when she is filled with God's spirit and draws the neighborhood around her in an electrifying communal experience of God's presence. Her connection with the pure energy of God's spirit is not mediated by what Spero calls anthropocentric God representations— the images of God shaped through formative experiences with others. She appears to have a direct connection with God.

Something that can enhance or interfere with direct apprehensions of God's presence and the subsequent formation of theocentric God representations is the projection of our internal representations of God onto others, the world, and God.[6] We see how easy it is to distort our experience of God by referring to Iris Murdoch's novel *Nuns and Soldiers.* When Anne Clavidge begins to feel the first stirrings of anxiety in the convent, she could have used her religious tradition to understand her anxiety as a separation from God and a form of sin. Instead, she senses that God is calling her to leave her home. Her abbess, like Anne, is open-minded about the sources of Anne's anxiety. Together they begin a process of discerning where God is and what Anne should do next.

Their faith system allows for a remarkably open attitude toward God. A vivid example of the ways in which a faith system can distort people's relationship with God is described by Philip Greven (1990), where scripture is used to justify corporal punishment of toddlers and young children. Children raised in strict, Protestant homes where corporal punishment is understood as a God-given means of child-rearing will internalize the religious systems of their parents and religious community. Biographies and autobiographies written by Protestant evangelists often describe the childhood experience of corporal punishment and at the same time try to justify faith systems that advocate child abuse. These faith systems depict an overpowering God who demands obedience through fear and the infliction of pain (Greven, 1990). This demanding God may take the form of a "monstrous superego that devours life instead of transforming it" (Vergote, 1988, 62).[7]

While object relations theorists imply that our most potent internal representations come from early childhood, more recent theorists have suggested that we continue to form potent object representations throughout our lives (Shengold, 1993). Transformative life events can change existing images of God, self, and significant others and add new images of God, self, and others. This potential for change was made vivid to me in research on the conscious God representations of women who had been abused as children (Doehring, 1993b). In this exploratory study, I measured the correlation between the severity of childhood traumatization and women's conscious God representations. I was looking specifically at childhood experiences of physical and sexual abuse and witnessing of domestic violence. In terms of God representations, I measured women's images of God as loving, observing, absent, or wrathful. I found that among the women in my sample,[8] conscious God representations remained predominantly loving even when there was traumatization and a high degree of traumatization in childhood. It was only when childhood traumatization became severe that their God representations became predominantly absent and wrathful. One way of understanding these findings is that these women may have been able to "work through" childhood experiences of abuse and arrive at a place where they experienced God as predominantly loving. They were able to salvage redemptive, beneficial aspects of their childhood experience of God, and as adults combine those with redemptive, nurturing experiences of God. Several women, when they began the God representation tasks, asked whether they should draw upon their childhood or their adult experience of God, and commented that if they drew solely upon their childhood experience of God, their choices would be quite different. This suggests that their predominantly negative or ambivalent images of God in childhood had been transformed into predominantly loving images of God in adulthood.

In reflecting on the constellations of internal representations of self, God, and others, it is important to realize that we can't reduce our personalities to a few constellations (loving mother-beloved child; proud father-proud child; loving God-child of God). The more attentive we are to our dreams and the complexities of what goes on in our internal world, the more constellations of internal representations we glimpse. An analogy might be our difficulty seeing much of the night sky when we are in a city, as the lights of the city obscure the light of the stars. When we are in more complete darkness, we can see a sky crammed full of stars. Using this metaphor, we can appreciate how we may only glimpse one or several images of mother and ourselves when a plethora of images exist in the unconscious.

God representations can be understood as the core of one's espoused and/or operational belief system. An important dimension of ministry (whether one is functioning as pastor, priest, educator, or preacher) is to be sensitive to the critical role of God representations in intrapsychic, familial, communal, and cultural systems. Our theological task is to monitor these God representations in terms of the extent to which they are part of disengaged, merged and overpowering relationships with God and others. For example, in reflecting on John Updike's character Tom Marshfield, I noted the ways in which his image of God as creator was intertwined with his need to overpower women sexually. This was apparent in the ways in which he experienced God as a rival in his relationship with a parishioner,

Frankie Harlow. If he could break her faith, then he and not God would be all-powerful. His images of God are part of his power struggles, which result in violence. Confronting him is a way of "taking on the gods" (Jordan, 1985) that rule his life.

Our theological task is to monitor God images in terms of the relationships implied in our images of God—specifically the ways in which power dynamics and relational boundaries interact in these relationships. McFague's model of metaphorical theology offers a helpful framework for this task of monitoring. She suggests that all theological models begin with a metaphor of what or who God is like. If the metaphor is rich and complex, it can become the seed for a model of God. According to McFague, a model draws upon both metaphorical language, which is primary, and conceptual language, which is secondary. Metaphorical language "feeds" conceptual language, while conceptual language "disciplines" metaphorical language. Metaphorical language divorced from conceptual language is "blind" and conceptual language without metaphorical language is "sterile" (McFague, 1982, 26). Models have the power to be transformative and revolutionary when they widen our vision to take in new possibilities. Models of God can become idolatrous when they are identified with reality. When presumed to be true for all people everywhere, models of God can not only be irrelevant but can also become oppressive.

When monitoring whether images of God are part of empathic and empowering relationships or part of disengaged, merged, and over-powering relationships, we can use a variety of pastoral theological perspectives. Poling and Graham elaborate pastoral theologies that draw upon process theology and assert that "everything that exists in the universe has come into being as a result of an interacting process" (Graham, 1992, 50). A liberation theological perspective, used by some African American, feminist, and Asian pastoral theologians, attends to power dynamics at a social level. Feminist theologies that take a post-structuralist perspective are helpful in elaborating the ways in which our theoretical perspectives can in and of themselves become disengaged, and can name reality in a way that is potentially overpowering. Process, feminist, and liberation theologies will provide helpful conceptual models for monitoring our images of God and the ways in which these images describe relationships that are empathic and empowering, or disengaged, merged, and overpowering.

In order to elaborate how one would engage in this theological task, I will consider God representations that describe a variety of relationships with God, including images of a God who is overpowering and disengaged, overpowering and merged, underpowered and disengaged, and underpowered and merged. I will sketch these various, potentially limiting relationships with God as a way of illustrating the usefulness of monitoring power dynamics and relational boundaries in our relationship with God, especially during formative and transformative experiences.

IMAGES OF A DISENGAGED AND OVERPOWERING GOD

I was raised in the Roman Catholic Church. As a child I took to heart the teachings of the church, and gave a legalistic and punitive emphasis to the rituals and catechism. For example, the only aspect of my preparation for my first communion that I recall was that the host was holy. This caused me to imagine all sorts of dire consequences if I chewed on the host, or if the host for whatever reason were to fall out of my mouth!

As a child I experienced priests and nuns as remote and overpowering.[9] In the schools I attended, I was aware of the threat of corporal punishment. My only encounter with the nun who was in charge of my elementary school was her seemingly cold, judgmental presence when I was twelve and was called down to her office for yet another interview with the police after I was assaulted.

These formative relationships became internalized and formed a constellation of intrapsychic images of myself, others, and God. At the center of the constellation was an image of myself as guilty and frightened. This was paired with images of punitive nuns, huge first grade teachers, and priests hidden behind confessional screens. The internalized figures were charged with feelings of fear and guilt and became one source of my images of God.[10] In contrast to this malevolent experience of school and church was my experience of singing in the school choir, and later taking out and reading books from the school library. Music and books put me in a world ordered by beauty and not fear. Looking back, I can see the way an empowering, empathic God became known to me through music and literature.

Many years later when I was seeking ordination in the Presbyterian Church in Canada I sometimes experienced those examining me for candidacy as a supreme court of black-robed judges sitting on high. My childhood images of religious authorities were recast in a Presbyterian form. It was hard to speak positively about myself and my call to ministry when I was transferring these exaggerated childhood figures onto the assorted men and women asking me questions about my faith and my call to the ministry.

Images of God as disengaged and overpowering have often predominated the hymns and preaching of the church. The well-known hymn, "Immortal, Invisible God Only Wise" describes God as "remote, inaccessible, hid from our eyes." Jonathan Edwards, a seventeenth-century preacher, in his sermon "Sinner in the Hands of an Angry God," depicts the sadism of a judging God who views sinners as powerless, inferior, and despicable. He elaborates the image of God's relationship to the sinner as someone holding a spider over the fire.

The difficulty with lifting out images of God from hymns and sermons is that we may have little awareness of the cultural context in which these hymns were written and sung. Jonathan Edwards preached to American settlers struggling to survive in a dangerous, often fatal environment. In this experience of being immersed in overwhelming chaos, immigrants may have needed to describe God as all-powerful. Unfortunately, Edwards then identified sinners with the chaotic, seemingly godless land. Similarly, people experiencing brutal oppression may describe God as all-powerful, the earth as harsh and cruel, and deliverance from earthly life as their only hope. Given their context, these people may have experienced some sense of empathy and empowerment by describing God as overpowering. This raises the question of who can judge God images and the relationships they depict. The person "inside" the relationship may describe feeling empowered by images of an all-powerful God. To someone outside of the relationship, their images seem to describe a power imbalance which not only limits their experience of God, but may have harmful consequences. Another difficulty with the task of monitoring power dynamics and relational boundaries in our relationships with God is that conscious images of God may be linked with unconscious images of God. What we see on the surface may be an espoused belief system;

what gets acted out may be an operational belief system involving different relational boundaries and power dynamics. Given these complexities, we need to approach the task of monitoring images of God cautiously, especially when our images of God are often precious to us and can feel like the heart of our faith.

Individuals who cope with traumatization through rigid God representations may find some sort of relief in preserving their parental and God representations as good, and in creating a world where strict punitive laws order life. For example, they may come to rely on images of an omnipotent, judging, punitive God consonant with fundamentalist religions.[11] Such religious systems[12] may serve as a protection against the primitive imagery of abuse which is experienced as demonic, and may create an external structure for the self. For example, a client associated images of God as father with her physically abusive father whose abuse often took her by surprise as a child. In trying to create order out of the chaos of violence, she constructed a complex rule system where she attempted to make violence predictable so that she could avoid "punishment." In her adult life she worked hard at creating the same rule system in her religion. She described overwhelming events as God "whacking her across the head." In spite of these negative images of God as father, she had positive representations of Jesus and used his name as a mantra that helped her relax and feel safe at night. In helping her to establish a sense of safety, the representations associated with God as father were not ultimately safe, while those associated with Jesus were.

Monitoring her images of God and Jesus can be a way of glimpsing her internal world, and the chaos she can experience. The more we are able to step into her shoes, the more we will realize the role of these images in creating order and safety. At the same time, the more we are able to stand outside her experience, and trust her relationship with God, us and those around her, the less fearful we may be of questioning or undermining particular images of God. Monitoring images of God has to be part of relationships in which we can glimpse the depths of another's world, our own world, and where God is. This is a highly contextual task that is embedded in particular relationships.

IMAGES OF BEING MERGED IN AN OVERPOWERING GOD

God has sometimes been portrayed as the merged, overpowering parent who is all-powerful and all-seeing, knowing everything that is going on. Listen, for example, to these verses from Psalm 139:1-4 (RSV):

> Thou hast searched me and known me!
> Thou knowest when I sit down and when I rise up;
>   thou discernest my thoughts from afar.
> Thou searchest out my path and my lying down,
>   and art acquainted with all my ways.
> Even before a word is on my tongue, . . .
>   thou knowest it altogether.

Theologies that emphasize the immanence and power of God, where God is wholly continuous with the creation, may stir up the anxiety of engulfment ("if I flee to the ends of the earth, thou art there"). We can contrast this anxiety about engulfment with the anxiety about abandonment that is stirred up when God is depicted as disengaged and all-powerful (Jonathan Edwards' image of God holding us like someone holding a spider by a thread over a fire describes the threat of disengagement).[13]

In recent years, feminist theologians have highlighted how disengaged our theology often is. In writing about the relationship between Christianity and sexuality, Ann-Janine Morey (1992a) comments on our long-standing difficulties with embodiment. Morey notes that we can celebrate the ways in which religion (or more specifically, a Christian religion) can regulate sexual relationships, but we become anxious when the power dynamics are reversed, and it is our sexuality which regulates our religion. It is clear that we feel comfortable when religion controls our sexuality, and quite uncomfortable when we see sexuality shaping, perhaps even controlling, our religion.

A difficulty with feminist writings on the inter-relationship of sexuality and spirituality is that they may not acknowledge the implicit power differential, and more important, they may not acknowledge what happens when we shift from disengagement into a fused or merged relationship. It is as if, in valuing our connections with one another, we lose the value of necessary boundaries. We no longer see the polarities of empathy: that it involves both connection and separation.[14] While not all theologies that emphasize embodiment and specifically eroticism share this same problem, there may be a tendency for such theologies to overemphasize aspects of eroticism that are like God. It may be difficult to identify power imbalances and merger inherent in some of these images of God.

Often images of God will arise in a particular context and may become generalized. This happens with Marshfield, where the particular context of serving communion to women he has sexually abused creates intense feelings and associated images of God that are used defensively as a way of denying his violent behavior. Another example of an image of God that arises within a particular context is found in Anne Marie Hunter's paper entitled "Numbering the Hairs on Our Heads: Male Social Control and the All-seeing Male God." Hunter begins by describing her work as a legal advocate for battered women and the stories she has heard about women being scrutinized, kept under surveillance, and sometimes stalked by their partners or ex-partners. From the particular experience of these women, she generalizes to the experience of all women, suggesting that every woman to some extent has experienced scrutiny, surveillance, and stalking from men—forms of intrusion and possessive control of women that are "an integral part of our cultural gender arrangements" (Hunter, 1992, 10). She likens this experience to Foucault's metaphor of how we are all being isolated and kept under surveillance in much the same way that prisoners without privacy are constantly watched by hidden guards. This grim image is used to describe the "normalizing gaze in medicine, psychiatry, education, religious institutions, the social sciences, and the military" (Hunter, 1992, 14). We internalize this gaze, and carry on a surveillance of ourselves. Hunter describes this as the male normative gaze that women experience and use to judge themselves. In a theological postscript to this paper, Hunter (1992, 23) suggests that the "God who numbers the hairs on our heads (Matthew 10:30, Luke 12:7), who knows us from our mother's wombs, who keep[s] [us] as the apple of his eye (Psalm 17:8), who watches over our going out and our coming in, our sitting down and our rising up" (Psalm 139:2) is an all-seeing, all-knowing God who may be experienced either as comforting or threatening, depending on whether this God's gaze is benevolent or malevolent. Hunter argues that women experience this all-seeing, all-knowing God as malevolent.

The difficulty with Hunter's argument is the tenuous link between the experiences of battered women who are stalked and all women, and the images of God that such battered women may have and the images of God that all women have. It makes sense that some women who are kept under surveillance might liken surveillance to descriptions of God's watchful gaze. To generalize to every woman's experience negates the highly unique experiences women have and the idiosyncratic images of God that are part of these experiences. To generalize along gender lines may also negate our experiences of God as an intrusive, overpowering mother (a more common image for a relationship with someone who is overpowering and who seeks merger). Jane Flax (1990, 1993) has commented on the tendency among feminists to idealize our connection with the all-powerful mother:

> Stories about mother-daughter relations reveal the recurrent power of our desire for a benign force or agent out there in the world looking out for us, attending to our needs, and ensuring their satisfaction. (Flax, 1993, 70) We want to be caught and held securely in an idealized mother's gaze. (Flax, 1993, 71)

The mother-infant relationship is seen as benevolent, and becomes the basis for images of an all-powerful God with whom we can merge, while the father-infant relationship is seen as a malevolent version of overpowering merger.

Again, what is missing in these descriptions is the particular circumstances in which such images arise. Momentary images of being held in the hands of God may be either comforting or terrifying, and may be an experience of empathy and empowerment or overpowering merger. Monitoring such images will involve attending to the particular contexts in which they arise, and attending to what may be below the surface in terms of what is absent or unstated in such images.

IMAGES OF AN UNDERPOWERED AND DISENGAGED GOD

We may be afraid that if we let go of a belief in God's omnipotence, God will become powerless—an irrelevant meaningless figure, disengaged and underpowered. This disengaged and underpowered figure is reminiscent of images of the crucified Christ. Rita Nakashima Brock describes some of the doctrines of the crucifixion:

> Doctrines of new life through the death of the son make separation and disconnection the source of reconciliation and connection . . . The doctrines of salvific death do not make sense. There is no mystery here. Connection cannot come from disconnection. (Brock, 1991, xiii)

If the crucifixion is understood as redemptive *because* Jesus experienced disengagement and was overpowered, then this suggests that disengagement and being overpowered are, in and of themselves, life-giving dynamics. In this way, women and men of faith have been encouraged to silently suffer with no resistance. Alternately, the crucifixion can be understood as redemptive because God was empathic and empowering even when Jesus experienced God momentarily as disengaged and himself as overpowered.

The process of scapegoating, another description of the crucifixion, can be described as an experience of disengagement and being overpowered. James G. Williams, elaborating the theory of Renée Girard, describes the way scapegoating is a hidden generative mechanism of human culture involving violent rivalry which is collectively controlled through selecting, isolating, and sacrificing a victim. Rivalry involves a contest to see who is more powerful. When such a contest threatens to become violent, the violence is turned toward a person selected to be the victim. The community becomes disengaged from the victim and then overpowers the victim.[15] Williams highlights the way the Hebrew and Christian scriptures ultimately uncover the victimization mechanism, favor the victim, and move against scapegoating toward fuller and fuller liberation from all sorts of victimization. Girard vividly describes the critical moment when the scapegoating process can be identified:

> Since the truth about violence will not abide in the community, but must inevitably be driven out, its only chance of being heard is when it is in the process of being driven out, in the brief moment that precedes its destruction as the victim. The victim therefore has to reach out at the very moment when his mouth is being shut by violence. (Girard, 1987, 218)

119

If the victim is empowered in this moment, then the community's disengagement may shift toward empathy, not only toward this victim but also toward others.

This is one way to describe the crucifixion and resurrection of Jesus. Though his body is killed, his voice is not silenced and continues to be heard among his male and female followers. It is his voice among them that resurrects their community and empowers them to become witnesses. Images of crucifixion which emphasize being disconnected and overpowered may ultimately reinforce relationships in which people are disconnected and overpowered. It is hard to imagine how such images of God can be life-giving. Sensitivity to the particular contexts of such images may help us monitor the life-giving and abusive potential of such images.

IMAGES OF AN UNDERPOWERED GOD MERGED WITHIN US

If we let go of a belief in omnipotence while having no sense of God as empowering, then God may simply become our own personal God. God will be powerless and merged in our own world. For example, those who pray when they need something in particular, such as a parking place, may envision God as *their* God, who is at their beck and call. Such images of God are of a God merged in their world. They are in charge and God (or so they imagine) follows.

It may be difficult to judge whether such images of God portray a God who is merged within and overpowered by us, or whether such images are part of a faith that is empowering and empathic. When called upon to put their faith into words, people may give individualistic images of God. Such images may appear at face value to be idiosyncratic in that they describe their God and no one else's. When such images appear to be trivial and sentimental then we might judge such images as merged and underpowered. However, if the fruits of faith are empathy and empowerment, then we might describe their theology as problematic and their faith as life-giving. Images of God, however simple on the surface, are embedded in complex and particular contexts. The more sensitive we are to these contexts, the more we will be able to explore the images of God that arise.

Sometimes highly idiosyncratic images of God can spring from an empathic, empowering relationship with God. Take, for example, some of the words of the eighteenth-century American hymn

"Jesus Christ, the Apple Tree":

> The tree of life my soul hath seen,
> laden with fruit, and always green:
> The trees of nature fruitless be
> Compared with Christ the apple tree.
>
> His beauty doth all things excel:
> By faith I know but ne'er can tell
> The glory which I now can see
> In Jesus Christ the apple tree.
>
> "Jesus Christ the Apple Tree"[16]

In the hymn, Joshua Smith describes sitting under the shadow of Jesus Christ the apple tree and how its fruit keeps his dying faith alive. This hymn, culled from a life experience, has a refreshing immediacy. The metaphor is not over-elaborated, but remains simple and direct. Another hymn describes the soul as a bird sailing toward eternal worlds:

> When for eternal worlds we steer,
> and seas are calm and skies are clear
> And faith in lively exercise,
> And distant hills of Canaan rise;
> The soul for joy then claps her wings,
> And loud her lovely sonnet sings,
> I'm going home.
>
> "When for Eternal Worlds We Steer"[17]

These hymns can be contrasted with those where a metaphor is so over-elaborated as to become sentimental. In such hymns, the over-elaboration of the metaphor suggests that God is reduced to the metaphor, merged in our world and overpowered by it.

IMAGES OF GOD AND POST-MODERN NEGATIVE THEOLOGY

Post-modern negative theology is the term used to describe a post-modern theology based on deconstruction.[18] The basic premise of negative theology is that if we attempt to name God, for example, as empathic and empowering, our very naming creates an overpowering doctrine. Negative theology is a stance of not naming: "God's name would suit everything that may not be broached, approached, or designated, except in an indirect or negative manner. Every negative sentence would already be haunted by God or by the name of God" (Derrida, 1992, 76).

Derrida was the first to link negative theology with post-structuralism, and he has continually resisted any systemic presentation of post-modern negative theology. When Derrida was invited to be part of a project whose aim was to engage his work on the topic of negative theology from both Eastern and Western perspectives, he declined to come and instead sent two papers, previously published at least twice (as Mark Taylor notes, 1992, 169). Morny Joy (1992, 261) describes Derrida's stance in his paper "How to Avoid Speaking: Denials" as an "avoidance of that resonant space that marks the inexpressible."[19] Derrida does not venture into the position of actually negating who and what God is.

The difficulty of the negative theology proposed by Derrida is the absence experienced when the author of creation and ultimate meaning is something about which we can no longer speak. David Jasper (1993, 5) describes negative theologians as attempting to encounter "the profound unknowability of the divine" by detachment. Derrida maintains that God is something that cannot be named because any naming will be logocentric: it will become an oppressive theoretical construction that limits and distorts who God is. The author/Author is declared off-limits to language, and in the process the center of faith is made into a black hole. Depicted in terms of the power dynamics and relational boundaries, the effect of this black hole is a dynamic of being underpowered and disengaged.

NEGATIVE THEOLOGY AND THE "BLACK HOLE"

Contemporary psychodynamic psychologists speak of the fragmentation of the self, self disorders, and difficulties in self-regulation as more common now than in Freud's time. Kohut links self disorders and fragmentation of the self with an absence of empathic relationships. The sense of a cohesive self, which Kohut suggests is formed developmentally through empathic parenting, has a regulating function for the personality, including the regulation of closeness and distance, with the threat of either the over-stimulation of merger or the isolation of disengagement.[20]

Focusing on how experiences of absence can disrupt self-regulation, Grotstein writes:

> The concepts of nothingness, meaninglessness, and chaos are informed by a deficit theory, a theory of "absence" . . . in addition to a conflict theory. It is my thesis that *conflicts* are to be resolved through *resolution* (dialectics) and that *deficits* are to be resolved through *self- and interactional regulation.* (Grotstein, 1991, 1)

Grotstein uses the image of the black hole to describe the chaos and meaninglessness associated with absence. He sees the source of this black hole to be a deficit in infancy, the:

> failure of the infant to impart (and to be helped by maternal [and paternal] containment and reverie to impart) meaning to the personal data of emotional experience causes it to default on its sense of self-authorization . . . disappear from the embodied self, and become an existential derelict, a cosmic vagabond. (Grotstein, 1991, 3)

Grotstein uses the terms *meaningless, disregulation,* and a *lack of self-authorization* to describe the severest character disorders. Drawing upon psychodynamic concepts like the holding environment (Winnicott, 1960) and the background of safety (Sandler, 1960), he suggests that infants require a "background presence of primary identification"[21] which acts as a backing for the emerging self. This background presence is provided by caretakers, and forms a primary experience of harmony with the world: "Ultimately the Background Presence of Primary Identification is *God,* the spiritual essence of our unknowable subjectivity" (Grotstein, 1991, 24).

One might speculate that post-modern dilemmas about naming God can induce a sense of absence, meaninglessness, and chaos similar in some way to the intrapsychic and inter-personal experience that Grotstein describes.[22] A refusal to speak about ultimate meaning combined with a refusal to be personally engaged might create a cultural black hole like the intrapsychic black hole Grotstein describes. Seen in this way, the absence experienced in post-modernism is not the absence created by a lack of meaning, but the absence of an empathic engagement with the author/Author. Without such an engagement there is no personal, ultimate meaning. Thus, the decentering effect of negative theology may be not in its refusing to speak of ultimate meaning, but in its refusing to speak of personal meaning and its refusal to be personally engaged.

Generally speaking, one can see three possible responses to Derrida's negative theological stance and the black hole (intrapsychic and cosmic) created by it. One response is to stand with him on the threshold, and elaborate a theology which describes absence in a way that does not invoke presence. A second response is to name some sort of indefinable, mystical, unknowable presence (for example, Morny Joy [1992, 263] uses the image of a wordless sanctuary to describe a negative theological perspective viewed through a "third" eye: a mystical eye of love). Anyone who does step in and propose such a theology risks taking a logocentric stance and risks being a pretender, that is, someone who negates only to confirm, as Morny Joy (1992, 278) notes. Despland alludes to the experiential quality of a negative theology when he suggests that negative theologies be thought of more as moments than as a systematic method or content. One function of negative moments in theology is corrective. A negative theological moment can illuminate both the unknowingness of God and the presumption of our claims to know God. Thus, negative theological moments correct the way we continually put ourselves in the center, in a logocentric position, when we presume to name God with words. In naming God we continually risk taking an overpowering stance and describing a God who is our god, an image of an underpowered god merged within our world. Taken this way, negative theological moments do not create black holes, but may instead create ways to correct for our need to overpower God and keep God merged.

I began this chapter by talking about empathic, empowering relationships with God. Reflecting on the ways in which particular images of God may imply merged, disengaged power imbalances in our relationship with God heightens our awareness of the complexity of our relationships with God. Glimpses of this relationship are difficult to judge, because what we see is so contextual and specific. In spite of these difficulties, we need to monitor power dynamics and relational boundaries in our relationships with God, because it is so easy for us to experience God in ways that are disengaged and merged, one-up or one-down. Given our alternating desires to have complete power over God and to give God complete power over our lives and our needs to be merged and then disengaged from God, we can appreciate how often we are pulled toward disengagement or merger, giving up or holding on to our power. Perhaps the best we can hope for are empathic moments, when we experience a true openness to God. Such moments can become touchstones for us. When Anne Clavidge, in Iris Murdoch's *Nuns and Soldiers,* is given a small, chipped stone by Jesus, this becomes a sign of the universe. Anne apprehends that she is like this stone, seemingly small and insignificant, but actually representing infinite possibilities. The stone becomes a touchstone, like the burn which remains unhealed, and invokes a sense of the as-if God and her own cosmic Christ. Our moments of being truly present with God can become touchstones, epiphanies that continue to guide us.

CHAPTER SEVEN

UNDERSTANDING SIN
AS DISENGAGEMENT, MERGER,
AND POWER IMBALANCES

W hen I worked as a pastoral care giver in a nursing home, one of the people I saw was an eighty-eight-year-old man. He was referred to me because he had become less and less involved in nursing home activities, staying in bed often during the day. The referral came in part because of the nursing staff's frustration with being continually called to his room when he was anxious. I began to get to know him as we talked about local politics. He had had a career in the entertainment industry and then had become involved in community work. Often when I arrived he would be feeling despondent. His mood would shift and he would become more animated as he told me about something he had heard on the news that interested him. I became more and more aware of the underlying loneliness and isolation that had been part of his life for a long time.

Gradually as our sessions continued, he became more interested in me. This interest suddenly became sexual as his difficulties with anxiety about his physical well-being intensified to the point of panic. He wanted me to meet him at a friend's apartment for a romantic rendezvous. He asked me questions about my physical appearance (what size did I wear, how much did I weigh) and wanted to hold my hand and stroke my arm.

In response to this sexual interest, I maintained professional boundaries while coping with feelings of awkwardness and anxiety. I set limits on his questions and physical contact. I told him that I couldn't be both his minister and a sexual partner, and that I was staying as his minister. His sexual attention reminded me of experiences during adolescence and young adulthood when I traveled on my own and had to cope with sexual attention from strangers. As a young woman far from home, my underlying fear was that something would happen to me and no one would know. Even though I knew that this situation was very different, I could not dispel my anxiety.

My re-experiencing of this anxiety made me aware of the forcefulness and intensity of this man's sexual attention. He seemed strong and powerful, as though he could get what he wanted. This was in vivid contrast to his ongoing experience of panic about his physical well-being and his feelings of helplessness and fear of death. Whereas he could be quite articulate when he focused his sexual attention on me, he had great difficulty putting into words the distress he experienced with physical pain and discomfort.

He asked me one day whether I had worked with young women in my ministry. He thought I would be a great help to them because I could model how to deal with men. He talked about how, in his years in the entertainment industry, he had often been attracted to university students and pursued them, and how some women could handle this and others couldn't. After this conversation, his sexual interest subsided and he became more and more immersed in his physical pain, anxiety, and panic. He died shortly thereafter.

His death made me more aware of one meaning of his sexual desire for me. I wondered whether he could feel less helpless and more powerful by trying to seduce me as he stood on the threshold of death. He was able to shift from feeling overpowered and merged in his approaching death to feeling disengaged from his pain and powerful in his efforts to seduce me. At one level I felt overpowered by this threat of being subsumed sexually. At the same time, my setting limits and listening and responding to the pain and fear at the core of his experience was a way of being empathic and empowering. I assume that these shifting power dynamics and relational boundaries occurred in his attempts to deal with death. He and I didn't have the opportunity to name what was going on within him and between us.

This story illustrates the need to monitor intrapsychic and interpersonal power dynamics and relational boundaries in pastoral care and counseling. If I had responded by becoming disengaged and overpowering, I might have neglected him. If I had felt so over-

whelmed by his sexual attention that I wasn't able to maintain boundaries, then I might have been abusive. I can broaden my understanding
of the ways power dynamics and relational boundaries interact by
considering some patterns of interaction: overpowering and disengaged, overpowering and merged, over/underpowered and disengaged, over/underpowered and merged. As I noted in the fifth and
sixth chapters, we can gain a deeper understanding of who we are as
pastoral care givers and counselors by reflecting on formative and
transformative events in our lives in terms of the ways in which power
dynamics and relational boundaries interact. The patterns of interaction I describe in this chapter may be helpful ways of understanding
what was painful about formative experiences.

SIN, DISENGAGEMENT, AND HAVING POWER OVER OTHERS

The need to have power over others while remaining disengaged
from what is going on within the other and within ourselves makes
us experience our bodies, the world, and others as objects that can
be taken and used. We can see this combination of disengaged and
overpowering dynamics in some of the images of health and maturity in Western culture in which independence is valued and
power is defined as winning battles and not as being energized by
reciprocal, mutual interactions. Our traditional definitions of sin
as pride, inflation, and alienation are based on this model of health
and maturity and the consequences of becoming too independent
and powerful. One existential anxiety underlying these definitions
of sin is the fear that we will become so disengaged that we will be
totally isolated, alone, and abandoned. These fears become acute
when we experience God as even more overpowering and disengaged than ourselves. Giles Gunn (1979, 181) notes this theme of
abandonment throughout American literature by men who have
"consistently depicted life's greatest terrors in terms of the imagery
of absolute abandonment."

The definitions of sin and existential anxiety that are formed out
of the experience of being disengaged and overpowering arise from
the typical experiences of those with power in our Western culture.
It is no surprise that such definitions are elaborated by Reinhold
Niebuhr and Anders Nygren. Until relatively recently these defini-

tions were taken to be transcultural and transhistorical. Valerie Saiving described an alternate understanding of sin: the experience of "triviality, distractibility, and diffuseness; lack of an organizing center or focus; dependence on others for one's self definition; tolerance at the expense of standards of excellence; inability to respect the boundaries of privacy . . . in short, underdevelopment or negation of the self" (Saiving, 1960, 109). What Saiving is describing is the experience of being underpowered or overpowered and merged: "depending on others for one's self definition."

Further examples of how sin has traditionally been defined in terms of being overpowering and disengaged are descriptions of destructive sexual desire. Alexander Irwin describes Tillich's understanding of sin as existential estrangement and "alienating concupiscence." Tillich contrasts the perverted desire that arises out of an estranged, prideful existence with the sexual desire intended in God's creation, which he calls essential desire and communion. He emphasizes that communion is not fusion but involves relational tension. In his descriptions of sexual desire as essentially good and in his emphasis on communion, he resonates with much of the feminist writings on erotic power.[1] Reflecting on his definition of sinful sexual desire, I can see the extent to which traditional moral and theological texts on sexual desire have focused on the experience of disengagement.[2] In these writings, there is little discussion of the woman, man, or child who becomes the "object" of "alienating concupiscence." Also, destructive sexual desire from a stance of being merged and overpowered is not considered.

Reflecting further on these needs to have power over someone or something while remaining disengaged, we can appreciate how these needs can arise in childhood experiences of wanting to radically separate ourselves from care givers who have power over us. Some have speculated that disengaged, overpowering dynamics may have their origins in childhood experiences of overpowering merger. Huston Smith describes this in terms of our existential fears of engulfment:

> In so far as we objectify our world by picturing it, it loses its power over us, for the move reverses our normal relation to it. Whereas formerly the world ruled us, beating our unconscious regions of our lives like waves on the shore they shape, now we rule the world, choosing which

picture of it to affirm and which to reject. This may sound like gain, which in autonomy it is, but there remains the disturbing issue of motivation. Can a life be as empowered by a world it intentionally selects as by one that feeds it from unknown, subterranean springs. (Smith, 1989, 48-49)

The inter-relationship of disengagement and merger is implicit in the definition of the verb *to disengage* as to "loosen from that which holds fast, adheres or entangles; to detach, liberate, free" (*Oxford English Dictionary*, 444). The engulfment which Smith describes in global terms can be restated in psychoanalytic descriptions of early child-hood development. The origins of the relationship between the disengaged and overpowering male and the engulfed subordinant female (or, according to Jessica Benjamin, the master and slave)[3] lie in early childhood.

> The anchoring of this structure [of domination] so deep in the psyche is what gives domination the appearance of inevitability, makes it seem that a relationship in which both participants are subjects—both em-powered and mutually respectful—is impossible. (Benjamin, 1988, 8)

A vivid illustration of the potential violence of a need to have power over another while remaining disengaged is provided by Milan Kun-dera in his book *The Unbearable Lightness of Being*. The narrator, Tomas, becomes disturbed by the way communist leaders were claiming their innocence, saying that they did not know what they were doing when they committed various atrocities in Czechoslovakia. Tomas uses the myth of Oedipus to say that if they could truly see (that is, empathize with) the suffering they had caused, they would, like Oedipus, be so distraught that they would want to put out their eyes. Not only did they "not know" the suffering they caused in the past, now, in the present, they were unwilling to see the full extent of this suffering. For if they did see and fully empathized, they would be overcome by horror. As Kundera illustrates, the "innocence" and "not knowing" of their disengaged stance was not an acceptable response to their sinfulness. They needed to shift to an empathic stance, and in so doing, truly put themselves in the shoes of those who had been overpowered.

130

The disengaged protagonist caught in a power struggle is a recurring figure in American literature. Giles Gunn notes the intrapsychic dynamics of a disengaged, overpowering stance in the protagonist, Captain Ahab, in Melville's *Moby Dick:*

> Melville's Ahab, for instance, experiences the "not-me," that "other" epitomized so completely by Moby-Dick himself, as a personal outrage, a gigantic affront to his sense of "me." Thus when the "not-Me," the "other," turns against him in a seeming act of vengeance, Ahab is driven into a fury of mind-annihilating hatred and rushes headlong to destroy it. (Gunn, 1979, 183)

Those who take a disengaged, overpowering stance are obviously disengaged from all those qualities they have devalued. Peter Rutter describes this from a Jungian perspective. He suggests that the intense sexual attraction a male therapist may experience for a female client is rooted in an attraction toward that which is devalued in himself, from which he is disengaged. The therapist's illusion that sexual intimacy will bring about healing is based on his intrapsychic need to be united with aspects of himself (like his own pain and vulnerability) which he projects onto his female client.

SIN, MERGER, AND HAVING POWER OVER OTHERS

The domineering and overinvolved parent has typically been described as the devouring mother who holds onto her children and won't allow them any room to separate or grow apart from her.[4] The potential for pathology in the mother-infant relationship has been all too fully elaborated among theories of the underlying causes of various psychopathologies. In psychoanalytic theory, mothers have been portrayed as the container in the depths of early childhood within which pathology is formed. One consequence of the mythic qualities of the mother's relationship to the infant and toddler is that mothers are not portrayed as actual people, but as a mirror, a container, and the object of desire. She is not presented as a real person beyond her symbolic role with the child. The portrait of merger between mother and child is such that mother is simply described in terms of the child's needs and world. What is missing in these descriptions of the mother-infant relationship is the role of mutual

131

recognition, in which not only the child's needs are recognized, but the mother's as well.[5]

Implicit in psychoanalytic theories of the pathological mother-child relationship is the terrible and absolute power of the mother over the infant. Dinnerstein suggests that patriarchy has been experienced as preferable to matriarchy because it is "a sanctuary from maternal authority" and "the mysterious . . . omniscience . . . of the nursery Goddess" (Dinnerstein, 1976, 176).[6]

Feminist writings on motherhood have re-valued women's roles as mothers. However, some feminists have fallen err to the same tendency to present the mother merely in a symbolic, albeit idealized role. As the father's overpowerment of the child has been denigrated by feminists, the mother's relationship with infant and young child, "the charmed preoedipal dyad" (Kahn, 1985), has been idealized and is "not only a magical moment for infant and early mother but exercises a charm over those who contemplate it, who study and theorize" (Gallop, 1987, 134). Gallop comments that feminists have tended to polarize mother versus father and pre-Oedipal versus Oedipal. She notes that "the tendency within feminist criticism to glorify the figure of the mother might often occur along with a concomitant pressure to cover over differences between feminists" (Gallop, 1987, 129). The pull toward merger is evident even in the way "the maternal figure may move many of us to wish for an embrace that obliterates otherness. And those of us who are attracted to psychoanalytic theory may be particularly susceptible to the mother's charming figure, the dream of the mother without otherness" (Gallop, 1987, 136).

French psychoanalytic feminists like Luce Irigaray, Helene Cixous, and Julia Kristeva have explored this pre-Oedipal mother-child relationship as possibly containing a form of discourse outside of the dominant discourse identified with the father. These explorations are within the larger map of Lacanian theory in which the symbolic father represents the order of language and law, rescuing the child from symbiotic fusion and engulfment in the mother. In contrast to a negative view of the mother's power, the French feminists describe this mother-infant symbiosis in terms of its immediacy, wherein referential language is not needed. Kristeva has described the discourse between infants and mothers as semiotic, a language without symbolic representation in which sounds are made purely for the joy of the sound (jouissance). Gallop has commented that the pre-Oedipal relationship between mother and child is often depicted as an innocent, joyful place where the intimacy between mother and child is such that referential language is not needed. The ushering in of the Oedipal triangle, with the looming ascendancy to power of the father is portrayed as the end of this innocent, blissful relationship.

This Lacanian perspective on early childhood may seem to many to be exaggerated, with its theory that language and the ordering of reality through language is identified with men (what Derrida has called phallogocentrism). This perspective does highlight the power of the dominant culture to name reality and even structure reality through its language. A broader understanding of the power of language and its collective metaphors is that we are all contained within language.

In her novel *The Edible Woman*, Atwood describes the role of culture in naming reality (in this case, what it means for a woman to become engaged). In her powerlessness to name any other kind of reality, Marian can all too easily merge with the dominant culture and its images, metaphors, and rituals of becoming engaged. From somewhere within her, though, a new language emerges: a language of images intertwined with physical sensations (her loss of appetite). This language ultimately empowers her to trust the reality she is experiencing.

It is clear that language and theory are often overpowering, not from a stance of disengagement, but merger. We are so fused with our language and theory that we cannot step out of them and see the ways in which we romantically blur our picture of reality (as Gallop says some feminists do when they look at the mother-infant dyad, and as Cushman says we do when we idealize attunement).

SIN, DISENGAGEMENT, AND BEING OVER- OR UNDERPOWERED

In the earlier reference to Milan Kundera's novel *The Unbearable Lightness of Being*, I described the way Tomas depicted communist leaders in Czechoslovakia. They claimed to be overpowered by their own ignorance, saying that they were innocent of any atrocities they committed because they did not know what they were doing at the time. A similar argument might be made by a parent who feels overwhelmed by a crisis or transition. Such parents might feel just as powerless as their children. In each of these instances, there is no larger familial, communal, or cultural system which steps in to take over. Ideally when a parent or community or even nation is overwhelmed and cannot provide adequate leadership, other family members, communities, and nations step in to act in empowering, empathic ways. When no outside help is available, then parents and others in authority may remain overpowered. The critical role of the larger community in intervening when parents experience helplessness is often blurred in cultures where individualism and privatism create the myth of the self-sufficient individual and nuclear family.

In experiences of abuse, a person in authority (for example, a parent, teacher, minister, or counselor) may *feel* inadequate and overpowered. When they are also emotionally disengaged from a child, parishioner, or client, they may also *imagine* that they have peer relationships with a child, parishioner, or client. For example, their conscious experience of sexual desire seems to be within a peer relationship, when in fact, their unconscious need is to have power over someone with less power than themselves. The "healing" which they identify with a sexual relationship is actually a way of compensating for feelings of powerlessness. If they were not disengaged from the other, and could actually put themselves in the shoes of the other, they would realize, first how harmful a sexual relationship is, and second that they are rationalizing their need for a sexual relationship with someone who is not a peer. Such rationalizations are: that children need sex education, that the sexual relationship can be discontinued without ill effect at any time, or that they have some talent for sex which makes them "healers."[7] It is critical to understand that though they may feel as if they have no power, they are in fact acting in an overpowering way. Also, when the larger community ignores or refuses to adequately intervene in such abuse, the community joins the abuser in being disengaged and overpowering.

These reflections on sin and disengaged, overpowered dynamics highlight the experience of those who *feel* overpowered, but who actually have power over others. A different experience of sin results from being disengaged from an aspect of ourselves because of fears of being overpowered by this aspect. We become separated from aspects of ourselves that are critical for a truly fulfilled life. An example of this is when we are disengaged from our own sexual desires and these lay dormant within us. This can happen when we have received ambivalent messages about our sexuality. Some women may disengage from their sexual desires throughout childhood and adolescence as a way of "being good." When they enter intimate sexual relationships, they may have little access to their sexual desire. It is something they have "turned off" so often within themselves that now they are unable to "turn on" these desires.

Others who have only experienced sexual desires (either their own sexual desires or the sexual desires of others) as overpowering may cope by attempting to disengage from their sexual desires. Anne Clavidge, a character in Iris Murdoch's novel *Nuns and Soldiers,* is an example of this. In university she experiences her sexuality as a carnival or maelstrom in which she is immersed. When entering religious life, she disengages from these sexual feelings. Upon leaving the convent, she again experiences the intensity of her sexual desires. There is a scene where she remembers what a demon swimmer she was in university, and realizes that when she entered the convent she thought she would never swim again. When she strips off her clothes and plunges into the sea, at first she experiences this as an exhilarating, sensual immersion in the movement of the sea. When the sea becomes too rough, she starts to drown and her friend Gertrude saves her.

Women may more or less "successfully" disengage from sexual desires as one way of coping with needs that are too dangerous. Generally speaking, women do not experience as urgent a need to act upon their sexual desires as men do.[8] Men may be more likely to attempt disengaging from sexual desires and then find themselves overpowered by these desires.

Experiences of disengagement from a life-giving dimension of one's self, followed by a sense of being underpowered because of this disengagement can be described as potentially sinful. Such disengagement may be in response to familial and cultural demands, particularly concerning what it means to be a woman or a man, heterosexual or homosexual, or from a particular ethnic group or religion. Sometimes the roles we assume—or which are imposed on us—demand conformity. In the process of conformity, we may disengage from any aspect of ourselves which does not "fit the role." Such a process of disengagement will inevitably interfere with our capacity for self-empathy and also our full potential for an empowering creativity.

SIN, MERGER, AND BEING OVER- OR UNDERPOWERED

The need to be compliant and accommodating contributes to what Winnicott (1960) called the False Self. This is the self we construct as a way of adapting to an external reality which we experience as overwhelming and in which we are merged. Some forms of pastoral care and counseling may unwittingly collude in the formation and maintenance of a False Self by helping us become more "functional" and increasing this adaptation to an overpowering external[9] reality. What Winnicott called the False Self contemporary theorists call pseudonormality, the "normopath," the "normatic" personality (an overview of these theories is given by Mitchell [1993]). For Winnicott, the sense of unreality that accompanies the experience of having a False Self comes from the absence of reciprocal relationships, involving a recognition that someone else's reality is different from one's own. The recognition of a plurality of realities is what shapes a sense of authenticity. The formation of a False Self arises when a person experiences only one reality, and with it a need to conform to that one reality. Illustrating this, Mitchell writes this of a client:

> In some fundamental way, she had never viewed her life as her own, to be shaped and valued according to her own interests, desires, and goals. Her own experience was hostage to her mother's vision of the world. (Mitchell, 1993, 23)

Mitchell describes the goal for his client as a "revitalization and expansion of [her] capacity to generate experience that feels real, meaningful, and valuable" (Mitchell, 1993, 24). In terms of power dynamics and relational boundaries, this would mean a shift from being underpowered and merged to being empathic and empowered.

For those in an underpowered position, merger (sexual or emotional) with someone who has authority may seem like a way to "get" the kind of power the person in authority seems to have. When those in authority do not act upon the "sexual" invitation of those who are seeking a false empowerment, a healing moment occurs (as Rutter, 1986, 250, notes). The more those in authority respond in an empathic (rather than a disengaged) manner to the "sexual" desires of the other, the more the other will experience self empathy and empowerment.

EMPATHY AND EMPOWERMENT

In elaborating the potential for sinfulness in terms of the interaction of power dynamics and relational boundaries, we can see the ways in which we can switch from one extreme to another. For example, the communist leaders described by Kundera shift from being overpowering and disengaged (when they committed atrocities) to being underpowered and disengaged (when they claimed they were innocent because they "did not know"). Similarly, those who disengage from their sexual desire because they feel overpowered by these desires (and this seems the only way to have control) may, in acting out these desires, shift to a stance of overpowering disengagement, particularly where others become the objects of their desires. A third example are those who experience being overpowered and seek a sexual alliance with someone in power as a way of regaining power. When those in power "reject" this alliance in a way that is demeaning and disengaged, then the original experience of powerlessness may be exacerbated.

In the process of monitoring power dynamics and relational boundaries, we will be less likely shift from one extreme to another. For example, Marian, the character in Margaret Atwood's *The Edible Woman,* allowed her "symptom" of not eating to become a language that helped her name her experience of feeling merged. Similarly, those artists who can vividly depict the experience of marginalization and powerlessness can, through their art, raise our awareness about power dynamics and relational boundaries so that we are less likely to remain caught in them. Writing on the occasion of Toni Morrison's receiving the 1993 Nobel Prize for literature, *Boston Globe* reporter Gail Caldwell said: "Morrison's early fiction not only authenticated the black experience by delivering the painful stories of a modern dispossessed, it also imbued these tales with a language so resonant it seems to belong as much to myth as to memory" (Caldwell, 1993, 16).

137

Sometimes the voices of the disempowered are silenced because they threaten to dismantle existing power hierarchies. This is what happens to Tomas in Milan Kundera's novel *The Unbearable Lightness of Being.* When Tomas writes an article likening the leaders of the communist party to Oedipus, he is told to either apologize or give up his profession as a doctor. He refuses to apologize and becomes a window washer.[10] Similarly, in Kundera's novel *The Joke,* the protagonist tells a joke that, through humor, discloses the power hierarchies of the communist regime. The protagonist is punished and finds his whole future altered by the joke he told.

The potential for language to either empower or overpower is explored by Elaine Scarry, in her book *The Body in Pain.* Scarry eloquently describes the way pain renders us inarticulate, in that we are often merged within and overpowered by physical pain. She notes how those who are not in pain have a limited capacity for empathy with the one in pain:

> When one hears about another person's physical pain, the events happening within the interior of that person's body may seem to have the remote character of some deep subterranean fact. (Scarry, 1985, 3)

This interpersonal disengagement is related to what Scarry calls the "unsharability" of pain and its "resistance to language" and further, the way pain "actively destroys language" (Scarry, 1985, 4). Those who work toward communicating the reality of pain are beginning what Scarry calls the collective task of diminishing pain. For Scarry, "the problem of pain is bound up with the problem of power" (Scarry, 1985, 12).

Another example of the critical role of language in monitoring power dynamics and relational boundaries is the role of language in expressing sexual desire. We may have difficulty talking about our sexual images, feelings, and experiences.[11] When these experiences are violent and there is nowhere to talk about what happened, then the absent family and community are aligned with the perpetrator.

We need a life-giving language to speak of our desires. Such a language distinguishes between consensual and coercive sexuality. Such a life-giving language is not pornographic and not simply technical but needs to resonate with the goodness and beauty of creation. We find examples of such language in love poetry like the Song of Songs. Such language is consonant not dissonant with the language we use to describe our spiritual desire.

In this chapter I have reflected on how power dynamics and relational boundaries interact to create potentially abusive relationships. The sequential way I moved from various interactions (disengaged, overpowering; merged, overpowering; disengaged, underpowered; merged, underpowered) seems to create clear categories in which to "put" our formative and transformative experiences. While this can initially be a helpful way to understand how power dynamics and relational boundaries interact, such categories may create a simplistic understanding of abuse and neglect. Given that there may be conscious and unconscious interactions of power dynamics and relational boundaries within not only the intrapsychic system, but also in the interpersonal, familial, and cultural systems, monitoring these dynamics is complex. How we name the interactions of power dynamics and relational boundaries may depend on what is going on within us, between us and around us.

For example, when I read John Updike's novel *A Month of Sundays,* I named what was going on at different moments in the book as abuse. Many others have read this novel and described it as a comedy, as a novel about communication, or as a description of the tension between sex and religion that has long existed in the United States. When we monitor power dynamics and relational boundaries, we bring our own unique perspective, which is shaped by our intrapsychic, interpersonal, familial, and cultural systems.

The risk in naming power dynamics and relational boundaries is that naming may become a way of having power over someone or something within our intrapsychic, interpersonal, family, and community systems. For example, a minister who tells a widow that she seems to be frozen in her grief may well be experienced as intrusive and presumptuous. Monitoring relational boundaries and power dynamics is not about coming to conclusions on our own and naming these conclusions as if they are reality. It's about listening, paying attention, and checking out in a variety of ways what we are experiencing, so that together we can create tentative meanings. For example, I may be telling my supervisor about a clinical experience where I felt overwhelmed and coped by shutting down and withdrawing. As my supervisor and I talk about this, the same dynamic may occur:

perhaps one of us or even both of us may start to feel overwhelmed and shut down. Given the interconnections between clinical relationships and supervisory relationships, it is not surprising that dynamics in one relationship can be replayed in some form or another in the other relationship. This means that even as we are monitoring power dynamics and relational boundaries, we are experiencing them and participating in them.

Throughout this book I have suggested that our moments of empathy and empowerment can illuminate disengagement, merger, and power imbalances. However, such moments are not completely reliable. For example, in John Updike's novel *A Month of Sundays,* Tom Marshfield writes that "the scales fell from his eyes" in a conversation with the organist Alicia. This seems like an epiphany, yet Marshfield does not suddenly become aware of his disengagement and need for power. What happens in this moment is that Marshfield shifts from being disengaged to seeking sexual possession. He writes that the moment of revelation happened in Lent, and by Eastertide they were sexually involved. Marshfield's isolation (he has no relationship that involved reciprocity, mutuality, and accountability)[12] ensures that whatever he names as true will remain unchallenged.

The categories of interacting power dynamics and relational boundaries which I describe in this chapter are intended as ways to begin a conversation with others. Monitoring needs to be done with others, honoring the complexity of our relationships, the limitations of our perspectives, and the power dynamics and relational boundaries formed by our very talking about these dynamics.

CHAPTER EIGHT

USING LITERATURE AS CASE STUDIES

As if the rubies and emeralds were clarifications of the ores, moments of intelligence that crystallize like insights in the middle of some dumb, dense love problem when the heat is really on. (Hillman, 1983, 191)

This image of jewels can be used to describe moments of epiphany: hard-won moments when the raw, heavy pain of our experience becomes transformed. When pain is described in terms of power struggles in which we are pushed toward merger and disengagement, an epiphany can be described as the moment of delicate balance when we experience empathy and empowerment. Such moments have a transparent and self-transcendent quality. We are able to see within and beyond the limited horizons of our experience and glimpse our world in new ways.

In this chapter I would like to use the metaphor of horizons to further explore the ways in which power imbalances and the pull toward disengagement and merger keep our horizons firmly in place. Moments of empathy allow us to look beyond our own horizons and see our own experience and others' experience in new ways that empower us. Charles Gerkin, drawing upon the hermeneutical approaches of Schleiermacher, Dilthey, and Gadamer, describes pastoral care and counseling this way:

> Pastoral work virtually always involves tending this dialogical relationship in which the particularity of the situation at hand and the horizon of meaning contained in the Christian story become open to reassessment, reevaluation, and reinterpretation. Attending to this dialogue is therefore best described as a hermeneutical (interpretive) task in the double sense of interpretation of core images and metaphors of the Christian tradition and interpretation of the particularity of contemporary situations with which the pastor is confronted. It is by means of

this process that, following Gadamer, I would label as *fusion of horizons* of those two interpretations that pastoral work can best be grounded in the core meanings of the Christian narrative of the world. (Gerkin, 1991, 19)

Pastoral care and counseling experiences often begin with story-telling. For example, when a family member dies, our first contact after the death usually begins with the story of the death. In exploring the story of death, there is often a sense of moving beyond the initial horizons of the story. When the minister meets with the family, the story of how the person died often moves people into the retelling of many stories about their relationships with this person, as the spouse, sons, daughters, visiting neighbors and the minister all talk about what they remember. In the midst of these stories, the minister and family may refer to where God is, and what hymns and scripture readings help them describe who this person was. As the family and minister talk, there is a "piling up of stories" (both conscious and unconscious, articulated and unarticulated). Some of these spoken and unspoken stories will be biblical stories about God's covenant with us. As these stories accumulate, certain meanings and images will emerge (Gerkin calls these meanings the uncovering of the deep narrative of the soul). The circle of family and friends reach a resting place where they feel as though, for the moment at least, they can make sense of this life and death. Often the hymns, readings, prayers, and sermon of the funeral service will be rooted in the deep narrative of the soul that emerged during pastoral care visits. The horizons of meaning shaped by the words and music of the funeral service will reflect the fusion of horizons that evolved as the stories "piled up" during pastoral care visits.

Walter Brueggemann, in *Texts Under Negotiation,* suggests that people change when "new models, images, and pictures of how the pieces of life fit together" evolve. This evolution is a "slow, steady process of inviting each other into a counterstory about God, world, neighbor, and self" (Brueggemann, 1993, 24-25). The counterstory creates a new horizon which becomes the container for a "new world, new self, new future" (Brueggemann, 1993, 25). This new creation happens through an accumulation of timely, particular transformative moments:

It is given only a little at a time, one text at a time, one miracle at a time, one poem, one healing, one pronouncement, one promise, one commandment. (Brueggemann, 1993, 25)

Transformation is most likely "in the moment of subversion where we are quite unsure, we are betwixt and between" (Brueggemann, 1993, 91). He borrows Victor Turner's concept of liminality to describe these moments when we are "between old configurations of reality and new models of reality" (Brueggemann, 1993, 91).

It is a moment of deep ambiguity that must be hosted with respect, awe, and patience, not rushed, not precluded, nor preempted. It is that precious moment of liminality that makes serious change possible. (Brueggemann, 1993, 91)

One may describe the counterstory as the story of "our being held in God's memory" (Patton, 1993, 6). This lovely phrase can be used to describe the horizons of meaning shaped by biblical stories of God's relationship with us which become like the background of safety (Sandler, 1960), the holding environment (Winnicott, 1960), and the Background Presence of Primary Identification (Grotstein, 1991)—psychological terms for the role that parents have for infants and young children. This grounding in the counterstory allows us to care for one another:

Human care and community are possible because of our being held in God's memory; therefore, as members of caring communities we express our caring analogically with the caring of God by also hearing and remembering. (Patton, 1993, 6)

When we experience being held in God's memory, the precious moment of liminality becomes transformative and not a black hole of chaos and meaninglessness. In terms of power dynamics, liminality is an openness to creative energies that is possible because we have let go of a need to either control or be controlled by someone or something.

In this chapter I will draw upon the hermeneutical and contextual approach to pastoral care and counseling to consider the use of literature as case studies. Often in case studies the clinician casts himself or herself in the role of omniscient, disengaged observer, with the client portrayed as someone either overpowered or underpowered by a morass of psychological difficulties in which he or she is merged. Such case studies are founded on two premises:

> The premise that the therapist knows better, sees more maturely and deeply into the patient's difficulties and into the very nature of life [and] the premise that the analyst's vision is a rational antidote to the chaotic, infantile, illusion-bound hopes and dreads of the patient's emotional inner world. (Mitchell, 1993, 17)

Case studies are often reductive. The complexity of a client's history is reduced to whatever constructs the clinician uses to make sense of his or her work. In more recent clinical literature, there is a growing awareness of the clinician's involvement in the therapy, and how the case study is as much a narrative about the clinician as the client. The perspective that evolves throughout the therapeutic work is understood as co-created by the uniqueness of the therapist, client, and their relationship. Given the complexity of conscious and unconscious layers of this co-created reality, any case study will only give us glimpses of what is happening.

In this chapter I would like to explore more fully the benefits of creating case studies out of literature by highlighting the ways in which the world of the novel both does and does not overlap the internal world of the reader. The right degree of overlap between the internal world of the reader and the world of the novel can create what Brueggemann calls the moment of deep ambiguity, with its possibilities for creating new horizons. When there is too little or too much overlap between the world of the novel and the internal world of the reader, the novel can exacerbate disengaged and merged dynamics, and contribute to the reader's horizons becoming inflexible.

Of course, novels are not written for the sole purpose of inducing liminal moments. When I create case studies out of novels and describe the potential for novels widening our horizons, I take a pragmatic and moralistic approach to art. I will highlight the limitations of such an approach to art toward the end of this chapter. Once we are aware of the limitations of this approach, we can be more attentive to honoring the artistry of the novel and to not using novels to create horizons of meaning that become oppressive.

THE BENEFITS OF USING LITERATURE AS CASE STUDIES: LITERATURE AND ITS CAPACITY TO INDUCE LIMINAL MOMENTS

One of the reasons we read fiction is to expand our immediate experience of the world, to know it intimately through the eyes and minds of strangers. (Moss, 1977, 55)

Fiction immerses us in the complexity and richness of another's world in a way unlike most clinical case studies. In the process of reading, we "take in" aspects of the novel and it is as if these become part of who we are. We can summon up these stories and use them to make sense of the experiences of others. For example, when I become immersed in the world of Holden Caulfield by reading *Catcher in the Rye*, I can experience what it is like to be a young man from a particular class and ethnic background in the sixties. Fiction can also increase self empathy. Like a prism that gathers light from all directions, a literary work can gather the diffuseness of our complex, layered experience. The story of another has the potential to gather up fragments of our own experience and present them in a narrative that is illuminating. Our horizon of meanings widens and we can enter more deeply into aspects of our own experiences and the experiences of others.

Literature has the capacity to widen horizons not only in individual readers, but also through the formation of empathic communities. Detweiler suggests that literature can sometimes provoke "a compassionate reaction of mutual care and concern . . . creating a community of response" (Detweiler, 1989, 27). He is realistic, however, about the reality of this happening in a "society that sets great store by individuality and privacy, that is attracted to *fictions* of communality which substitute for actual shared public life, that nurtures with some nostalgia the myth of the ideal story-telling community but does little to realize it" (Detweiler, 1989, 33).

In reflecting on fiction's capacity to widen our horizons,[1] it is helpful to return to some of the polarities of empathy (presented in chapter 5): (1) being both subjective and objective; (2) understanding (going deeper into) and explaining (gaining an overview); (3) drawing upon knowledge gained from being connected with and separate from the other; and (4) doubting and believing (Schlauch,

145

1990, 8). When there are imbalances among these polarities within the reader, reading fiction may reinforce disengagement or fusion. I will consider each of these extremes, beginning with fusion.

When there is an almost complete overlap between our internal world and the world of the novel, fusion may result. Such consonance between our internal world and the world of the novel may be soothing, but it may simply confirm the horizons of meaning we already have. The example of this that comes most readily to mind is the Harlequin romance novel. If my internal world is filled with images of mysterious, tragic, powerful males who will sweep me passionately off my feet, then I will find this internal world mirrored in the Harlequin romance, with its doctors, professors, or country squires and nurses, students, or governesses whose stormy relationships become enflamed with passion. Another example is the genre of adventure stories located in the "Wild West." The male reader of such novels may easily identify with the cowboy who saves damsels in distress, has shoot-outs with outlaws, and indulges in barroom brawls. My examples may sound sexist, in that I speak of women readers when I refer to Harlequin romances and male readers when I refer to adventure stories. These examples illustrate the ways in which gender may be an important factor in choice of literary genres. Both types of fiction to which I refer rely upon stereotypic gender roles which may make these novels comforting for readers.

The most disturbing example of fusion between the reader's internal world and the world of the novel is the way in which a sexually and/or physically violent video can mirror the internal world of the viewer. This example leads us to question whether this mirroring actually results in abuse or neglect. Some argue that the cathartic effect of this fusion makes it *less* likely that people will act upon what they read or see, and *more* likely that they will separate out reality from fiction. A recent discussion of the relationship between what we view on the screen and what we do to others concerned the video "Child's Play 3." This video was discussed at the British trials of the two ten-year-olds who beat to death a toddler, James Bulger, and the group of teenagers who kidnapped, tortured, and set fire to a teenaged female acquaintance (Martin Amis, 1994). That the video mirrored the internal worlds of these children and teenagers seems self-evident. How it was part of their acting upon their fantasies is not clear. I highlight this discussion not to provide any ready answers but to note the very disturbing contexts of such discussion. The difference between what goes on in the internal world of these children and teenagers and their decision to act upon their wishes and fantasies remains critical in the discussion of the connection between fusion and abuse.

At the simplest level, a consequence of fusion between the internal world of the reader and the novel is that reader's horizons of meaning remain unchanged and this may mean that fusion with and disengagement from others continues.[2] When the novel simply resonates with our internal world without any dissonance, the novel loses its potential to induce liminality: the experience of being between one's old horizons and the emergence of new horizons. One's "self-aggrandizing and consoling wishes and dreams . . . prevent one from seeing what is there outside of oneself" (Murdoch, 1971, 59).[3] We are not able to see what lies beyond the horizons of our internal world and the novel which mirrors our internal world. Such "not seeing" can result in disengagement. An example are the many, many American novels that are populated only by Euro-American characters. Toni Morrison (1992) pays attention to the presence or absence[4] of black images and people in American literature. Most often the presence or absence of these images and people simply reinforces the culture's *disengagement* from the humanity of black people and *fusion* with the stereotypes they project onto blackness. What she finds remarkable is that literary critics themselves do not notice and remark upon the presence or absence of black images of people. Morrison argues that the way black images and people are referred to in fiction and literary criticism has been part of a need to maintain overpowering dynamics. The disengagement and fusion of authors, readers, and critics is rooted historically in the fear of newly arrived Euro-American settlers. Morrison eloquently describes this fear:

> Americans' fear of being outcast, of failing, of powerlessness; their fear of boundarylessness, of Nature unbridled and crouched for attack; their fear of the absence of so-called civilization; their fear of loneliness, of aggression both external and internal. In short, the terror of human freedom—the thing they coveted most. (Morrison, 1992, 37)

Morrison understands the important role of novels in helping people encounter and not evade these fears (a process she calls "romancing the shadow").

Judging the extent to which the novel simply mirrors the internal world of the reader can also be a way of judging the art of the novel. Murdoch (1971, 59) goes so far as to say that "almost anything that consoles us is a fake."[5] In other words, when the world of the novel simply mirrors our internal world, then it is no longer "beautiful." Murdoch alludes to the dynamics of merger when she says that the truly beautiful is " 'inaccessible' and cannot be possessed" (Murdoch, 1971, 59).

> Great art teaches us how real things can be looked at and loved without being seized and used, without being appropriated into the greedy organism of the self. (Murdoch, 1971, 65)

In other words, great art resists becoming submerged in our world. This discussion of the way in which we can take an overpowering merged stance toward what we read and appropriate it for our own uses parallels an earlier discussion (in chapter 6, "Images of an Underpowered God Merged Within Us") of the way in which we want to have a highly personalized relationship with God where we are in charge. The adjectives Murdoch uses to describe the differences between "fake" and "truly beautiful" art may also be used to describe our images of God.

Having considered the ways in which too much consonance between our world and the world of the novel induces not liminal moments, but rather fusion, we can turn to the experience of having too little consonance between our world and the world of the novel. Dissonance is created by the ways in which our world is separate from the world of the novel. Such dissonance can make us reshape our horizons of meanings, to make sense of what is dissonant. Often a novel's dissonance

> brings the reader up short, shatters his or her expectations, to unveil (Heidegger) or disclose (Ricoeur) a deeper awareness which derives from the text's world . . . turning inside out and, as it were, inquiring of the reader, asking the reader the question of *his* or *her* horizon. (Arnold, 1993, 114)

If there is too much dissonance between our world and the world of the novel, we may simply remain disengaged from the novel. When the world of the novel feels inferior to our own, we feel disengaged and superior. This can happen when we read a novel describing a culture utterly different from ours which we judge as inferior. A less complacent experience is that of reading a novel from which we feel disengaged and which overpowers us. I had this experience in reading the novels of Brett Ellis. He describes sociopathic characters who torture and rape women. I wanted to experience no overlap between my world and the world of these male protagonists. What was most disturbing was to experience the overlap of my world and the worlds of the women who were attacked. I felt overpowered by the violence of his fiction.

Relational boundaries can be used not only to understand how fiction may or may not transform our horizons of meaning, but also how fiction may transform our understanding of God. Experiencing that part of the novel's world that does not overlap with our internal world can be called an experience of the other or otherness.[6]

Otherness is more than just the presence of difference; it is the presence of difference that cannot be reduced or eliminated. (Poling, 1991, 111)

Gunn argues that American writers have described the experience of and response to "otherness" in three ways. The earliest American writers, from the Puritan era throughout the first half of the nineteenth century, described the experience of the "Other" as the transcendent God, and their response was either to consent to or withhold consent from this God. In the mid-nineteenth century, those writing American literature began to describe the experience of otherness in terms of their experience of the people around them. The response to an encounter with the "Other" within those around them was what Gunn called sympathy: a projection of "ourselves so completely into the interiority of their distinctive inwardness that, as D. H. Lawrence once said, we 'feel with them as they feel with themselves.' "[7] This response to what is "other" or "not-me" seems to describe a form of merger, in that we take over the space of the other without letting the other into our space. As an example of such sympathy, Gunn describes the good works of Hester Prynne in Nathaniel Hawthorne's *Scarlet*

Letter. Prynne is highly responsive to those around her but does not let anyone into her world. The third mode of experiencing the "other" began in the second quarter of this century with "the discovery of the astonishing numinosity of things as they are" (Gunn, 1979, 205)—that is, in the world all around us. Our response to this numinosity (" 'otherness' in the immanental mode") "is neither consent nor sympathy but rather transparency" (Gunn, 1979, 206). While Gunn does not elaborate what he means by transparency, it obviously involves reciprocity and empowering, rather than overpowering, dynamics.

In reflecting on these evolving ways of relating to otherness, I note how much the experience of the other can evoke a shift toward disengagement, merger, and a power imbalance. For example, in identifying the other as the transcendent God, we create a power imbalance, with God seen as either disengaged from the world (where transcendence involves disconnection) or us seen as merged within a God whose immanence "invades" everything. Or, we might disengage from and denigrate that which is other. It is hardest to remain in contact with that which is other and seek some sort of empowering relationship where there is an exchange of energy. Poling (1991, 110-111) calls this the ambiguous self.

THE LIMITATIONS AND DANGERS
OF USING LITERATURE AS CASE STUDIES

A theoretical basis for discussing the limitations of creating case studies out of novels is provided by interdisciplinary studies of religion and the arts. In an excellent overview of this interdisciplinary study, Giles Gunn describes the first generation of such interdisciplinary studies as being in part interested in the educative or pastoral function of literary study. A problem with these early writings of the 1920s and 1930s was that they were "so accommodating to literature or art that one lost all sense of ethical and theological standards" (Gunn, 1979, 22). As a corrective, they needed to articulate "a theological position or set of religious norms at once more supple and capacious as well as precise" (Gunn, 1979, 22). The earliest interdisciplinary studies of theology and the arts highlighted the limitations of using theological models which are too simplistic. This raises a question: how supple and capacious is a model of the interaction between power dynamics and relational boundaries in providing a set of norms from which to reflect upon the intrapsychic, interpersonal, familial, and communal dynamics portrayed in a novel?[8]

In using fiction as case studies, I look at the power dynamics and relational boundaries present in the intrapsychic, interpersonal, familial, cultural, and communal systems depicted in a novel or short story. Using literature as case studies most closely conforms to a pragmatic approach to literature.[9] I use literature for a purpose: to illustrate the usefulness of a set of norms (the interaction of power dynamics and relational boundaries) for understanding when relationships are abusive. The great danger of a pragmatic approach, as Gunn (1979, 73-74) points out, is that the novels I use simply become a means to an end: "At worst, literature is turned into a form of propaganda or reduced to an object lesson" (Gunn, 1979, 74).

The sheer artistry of a literary work can be lost when literature is used as case studies. One way to offset this loss is to pay particular attention to the beauty of the text, and to use quotations that let us glimpse this beauty. Another way to appreciate the novel as an artistic work is to be familiar with and use the work of literary theorists. For example, in using the novels of John Updike, Iris Murdoch, and Toni Morrison, I converse with those who have written about these novels as a way of valuing the novel as a work of art.

The larger theoretic frame of these case studies is post-structural-istic, with the questions and answers raised in both post-structuralist theologies (like post-modern negative theologies) and literary theories. Post-structuralist approaches are helpful in highlighting further risks of using literature as case studies in order to analyze how power dynamics and relational boundaries interact to create potentially abusive relationships. This model, if assumed to be transhistorical, becomes as imperialistic as any modern theory. Within a *modern* frame, the model appears to be the key[10] which unlocks the meaning within the text—in this case, the pastoral theological meanings. Within a *post-modern* frame, the model may produce a relative, momentary meaning that is particular and not universal. When we lose sight of this post-modern frame, then there is a danger of reducing these stories to ideas. Trusting in the plurality of readings and the indestructibility of the story, I can venture my own readings of John Updike's novel *A Month of Sundays* (1975), Sinclair Ross' novel *As For*

Me and My House (1941), Toni Morrison's novel *Beloved* (1987), and Iris Murdoch's novel *Nuns and Soldiers* (1981).

There is another danger of moving unwittingly from a post-modern to a modern frame in using literature as case studies. When we approach novels as case studies with a modern and not a post-modern frame, we may create universals out of the particularities of these stories. The particularities of novels do create certain horizons of meaning in which we can understand our own experiences. These horizons of meaning are not transhistorical and transcultural. We can bring a hermeneutic of suspicion to the horizons of meaning we create out of these stories which I outline below:

1. There are *unconscious dimensions* to stories and novels which may never be named and which may be glimpsed in the gaps, inconsistencies, and instability of the novel. These unconscious dimensions may greatly shape the horizons of meaning created by the story or novel.

2. When we focus primarily on a novel's protagonist and his or her intrapsychic experience, we may be unaware of the degree to which his or her story is *shaped by his or her race, gender, and class.*

3. There are always *ideologies of race, gender and class embedded in the horizons of meaning created by a story or novel,* for example, stereotypes of particular ethnic groups. We as the readers may be "blind" to these ideologies and stereotypes, and unaware that our horizons of meaning are not only irrelevant but oppressive for those different from us.[11]

In this chapter I have explored the capacity of a novel to transform our horizons of meaning or exacerbate merger and disengagement. I have also considered the limitations, dangers, and needed safeguards of using literature as case studies. The complexity of the discussion highlights for me both the rich benefits and deep risks of undertaking any use of case studies, whether one draws from literature, clinical work, or personal experience. The benefits can be a widening of our horizons of meaning; the risks are increased disengagement, merger and a need to overpower.

CHAPTER NINE

MONITORING RELATIONAL BOUNDARIES AND POWER DYNAMICS IN PASTORAL CARE AND COUNSELING

In much of this book I have focused on the abuse that can follow when overpowering, merged, and disengaged dynamics interact in intrapsychic, interpersonal, communal, and cultural systems. The novels of John Updike, Sinclair Ross, Toni Morrison, Iris Murdoch, and Margaret Atwood, and the short stories of Raymond Carver illustrate what happens when we act upon disengaged, merged, and overpowering dynamics. We all experience the interaction of disengagement, merger, and power imbalances in our relationships. These dynamics occur not only within us, but within our families, communities, and culture, especially during crises and transitions that can potentially form and transform us. I have argued that we need to monitor these dynamics in ourselves, our families, communities, and culture. I have described the complexity of such monitoring. Often the best we can do is glimpse the ways in which power dynamics and relational boundaries interact. Our greatest clarity comes in moments when we experience empathic relationships, where there is an openness to and engagement with one another and a flow of energy that makes us receptive and pro-active rather than polarized in a power struggle. Monitoring power dynamics and relational boundaries is not a theory but a way of being in relationship. It is not something we can read about in a book and then go out and do, and it is not an individual task but a dialogical process.

When a minister and parishioner or pastoral counselor and client monitor the relational boundaries and power dynamics going on in the present and understand how these dynamics relate to past experiences, then attention will be given to anything that triggers disengagement, merger, and power imbalances. When they take into account not only intrapsychic and familial systems but communal and cultural systems, then they can understand how one's gender, class, sexual orientation, and other aspects of one's identity influence power dynamics and relational boundaries. For example, if Marian, the protagonist in Margaret Atwood's novel *The Edible Woman,* was someone we encountered in premarital counseling, we might work with her and her fiancé to understand how her difficulties with food were connected not only to her intrapsychic dynamics of feeling merged and overpowered by her new role as a fiancée, but also with the way her culture assigns her a new role that is constricting and confining and gives her no language to make sense of her experience other than saying she is experiencing premarital jitters.

By paying attention to the interaction of the relational boundaries and power dynamics that occur in the crises or transitions that bring people into pastoral care or counseling, we can together monitor the potential an individual, couple, or family has for abuse. Our attending to the interaction of power dynamics and relational boundaries can shift these dynamics so that power imbalances decrease and needs for disengagement and merger lessen. Shifting intrapsychic and interpersonal dynamics can make us experience God differently. For example, when Marian, in Atwood's novel *The Edible Woman,* feels submerged in her new role as fiancée, she may identify God with the confinement and constriction she experiences in the institution of marriage. When at the end of the novel she constructs a cake in the shape of a woman and then attacks it with gusto, she may experience a God who delights in her symbolic act.

Monitoring the interaction of relational boundaries and power dynamics is not simply an aspect of dyadic forms of pastoral care, but also a way in which communities of faith can provide pastoral care. Recent texts on pastoral care (for example, Patton's *Pastoral Care in Context* and Wimberly's *Pastoral Care in the Black Church*) highlight the role of the community in the pastoral care ministry of the church. In Toni Morrison's *Beloved,* we see an example of a community providing pastoral care. The elderly black man Stamp Paid realizes that the neighborhood has been disengaged from the household at 124 Bluestone Road with terrible consequences for Sethe and Denver. The women in the neighborhood also realize that something is terribly wrong in this household. As one of them says, sin has taken over—words that describe the interpersonal and intrapsychic battles going on within the household. The actions of Stamp Paid and Sethe's female neighbors are an example of community pastoral care that is grounded in a sensitivity to power dynamics and relational boundaries. What is particularly noteworthy about this example of community pastoral care is that it occurs in the midst of a larger racist culture in which freed slaves are continually dehumanized and made targets of hatred and violence.

When power dynamics and relational boundaries are monitored, our pastoral care and counseling relationships become containers for healing, sustaining, reconciling and guiding.[1] I would like to elaborate my understanding of the role of empathic empowering moments in pastoral care and counseling by suggesting that the "piling up" of such moments shifts pastoral care and counseling from a contractual to a covenantal relationship, and that the covenantal relationship becomes the container for healing, sustaining, guiding, and reconciling.

There are at least three important dimensions of the metaphor of pastoral care and counseling as a covenant: (1) the immediate contract that is established as care and counseling begins, (2) the outside contract shaped by the institutional and professional organizations within which care and counseling is contained, and (3) the implicit contract concerning power dynamics and relational boundaries, which becomes a covenant as moments of empathy and empowerment increase and relational boundaries and power imbalances are monitored. All of these dimensions of the contract are crucial in creating a covenantal container. I will consider the immediate contract, the outside contract, and the implicit contract in terms of how they establish a safe and potentially healing pastoral care or counseling relationship, or an unsafe and potentially abusive pastoral care or counseling relationship. Before considering the ways in which the contract becomes a covenant, I would like to highlight some of the differences between pastoral care and pastoral counseling.

DIFFERENCES BETWEEN PASTORAL CARE
AND PASTORAL COUNSELING

Pastoral care is essentially a supportive relationship in which the minister, administrative body, and congregation act in a supportive way to enable those in crisis and transition to grow in the midst of change. Bob Randell, using the psychodynamic theory of Heinz Kohut, highlights the importance of an attuned, empathic community of faith, and how we never outgrow our need for such relationships. The ordinary caring that a congregation gives to people in crisis and transition determines whether transitions or crises will be creative or destructive for individuals, families, and groups.

Sometimes individuals, families, or groups become "stuck" in the midst of a crisis or transition, and the crisis or transition becomes overwhelming and immobilizing. Getting stuck may involve several factors. *First,* the stressors of the particular crisis or transition may be overwhelming in and of themselves. For example, the death of a child is a very painful and complex loss to reconcile and accept. *Second,* the individual, family, or group may have a history of overwhelming life events which compounds the difficulties of the present crisis or transition. For example, a congregation with a history of troubled relationships with their ministers may find it more difficult to connect with new ministers and let go of departing ministers. *Third,* there may be particular vulnerabilities within the intrapsychic, familial, and/or group system which become potentially disabling in the present crisis or transition. For example, an individual or even a family or group may tend to become violent, depressed, anxious, extremely self-critical, or paranoid under stress. Such vulnerabilities will make it more likely for them to run aground when trying to navigate their way through a crisis or transition. *Fourth,* when overwhelming life events happen in childhood and adolescence, children and adolescents are at particularly vulnerable developmental stages in which they simply do not have the emotional, cognitive, and psychological structures to manage the crisis. Left without support, they will easily become stuck. *Fifth,* there may be an inadequate social support system that cannot provide the psychological and spiritual structures that facilitate containment in the midst of a crisis or transition. For example, when families lose someone through suicide, the church's silence about the meaning of this death will create an absent and not a supportive spiritual community in which suicide can be named and made sense of in terms of people's faith. *Sixth,* there may be social, cultural, and organizational dynamics that are part of particular transitions or crises which contribute toward, and may even create, the context for the transition or crisis being overwhelming. For example, when a congregation acts out its homophobia, it will make it exceedingly difficult for members who are coming out and publicly acknowledging their sexual orientation to navigate this transition.

When the stress of a transition or crisis becomes compounded by any of these six factors, then individuals, families, or communities can get overwhelmed in the midst of a crisis or transition, and the pastoral care provided by a community and pastor is no longer enough to help them navigate the turbulent waters. When this happens, then a referral to a pastoral counselor is needed.

As I have described pastoral care, it can be likened to the supportive role of a midwife, where the crises or transitions that people are going through are viewed as essentially life-giving, and pastoral care is the supportive presence that monitors what is happening. Pastoral counseling is called for when a crisis or transition becomes compounded and threatens to overwhelm people. Sometimes all that is needed is crisis intervention, and the minister and pastoral care community can step in more actively to help manage the crisis. When this is not enough, then careful and prompt referrals are needed.

In both pastoral care and counseling, the roles of what I call the initial contract and outside contract are critical in creating the covenantal relationship in which care and counseling occurs. I would like to explore each of these dimensions further and highlight as I go along the ways in which these contracts are different in pastoral care and counseling.

THE IMMEDIATE CONTRACT ESTABLISHED AS PASTORAL CARE OR COUNSELING BEGINS

Whether we are aware of it or not, pastoral care begins with a contract, usually unstated. When I go to the hospital to visit a parishioner, I am working upon a usually unstated agreement that I will call upon parishioners experiencing the crisis of hospitalization, and by my visit be present with them, in some degree or another. If I were to verbalize the contract I might say, "I am here to listen to what has happened, understand what this means for you and understand where God is in the midst of this crisis." Acting upon this unstated contract is what makes my visit a pastoral care experience, and not simply a social visit. We may become familiar with the terms of these unstated contracts in seminary when we learn about how to be pastoral care givers for those facing death, for couples preparing to marry, and for parents bringing children to be baptized. The nuances and details of the unstated contract will differ depending on what crisis or transition people are undergoing. As our pastoral identity is formed throughout our seminary experience and beyond, we are often implicitly shaping the terms of the pastoral care contracts that will make up our pastoral care ministry; for example, what sort of premarital counseling we will offer, or how available we will be to members of the church and community in the midst of particular crises. Sometimes conflict will surface when our implicit contract differs from those to whom we minister. A couple in the community may expect the minister who officiates at the wedding to also preside at the reception. They may consider this part of her or his role as a pastoral care giver; the minister may not.

The immediate contract at the outset of a pastoral care encounter can often be easily stated as a way of making known the purpose of a visit or meeting. Such statements can help us make the transition from the social exchanges that often open a pastoral care encounter to the concerns of our parishioners and the purpose of our meeting. At the end of the visit, we can talk further about what happens next; this is a way of contracting with one another again. In a culture where many parishioners may not understand the role of a pastoral care giver, making the contract as explicit as possible can be helpful. For example, when a minister ends a hospital visit by saying that he or she would like to call or visit next week when his or her parishioner is at home, this is a way of making clear what will happen next, in much the same way as a nurse might talk to the same person about the care they will need once they have returned home.

A minister may unwittingly shift from providing pastoral care to providing pastoral counseling when those in distress seem to need some sort of intervention because they are overwhelmed and stuck. This can happen during a visit to an individual, couple, or family in the midst of crisis when we implicitly or explicitly shift into providing crisis intervention. In the process, the original unstated contract to provide pastoral care may become a contract to provide pastoral counseling, at least for the duration of the crisis. The shift from pastoral care to pastoral counseling can happen without an assessment process being done and without a contract being negotiated. The parishioner who shifts to being a client will likely not be aware that her minister is now more like a pastoral counselor than a pastor. She may also not fully appreciate the need for an explicit contract, in which frequency, length, and fees of counseling sessions are negotiated. She may not be able to fully evaluate whether her pastor is actually qualified to provide pastoral counseling, and may not have the opportunity to choose him or her as her pastoral counselor. What this means is that the role of consent in the contractual process is absent. The parishioner has not been fully informed about the shift from pastoral care to pastoral counseling; the shift has taken place in a relationship in which she is vulnerable and may not be in a position to understand what is happening. It is the minister's responsibility to fully explicate the shift taking place, and provide the parishioner with all the information needed for her to give consent to beginning pastoral counseling.

Unlike pastoral care, pastoral counseling almost always begins with an explicit agreement about what is going to happen. Usually the initial contract involves talking together and assessing the crisis that has brought someone to us. In the assessment process, the pastoral counselor meets with an individual, couple, family, or group for time-limited appointments that have been made expressly for the purposes of assessment. During such a session or sessions, the counselor structures the meeting so that everyone involved can fully explore what the present problem is. Part of the assessment process involves the counselor's assessment of his or her own expertise and the availability of adequate supervision or consultation. Does he or she have the expertise and support to undertake working with this person, couple, family, or group? If the pastoral counselor assesses that she or he can provide the counseling needed, then a plan of care (what clinicians call a treatment plan) needs to be formulated and discussed with the individuals, couple, family, or group, and they need to understand the practical arrangements of time, place, duration, and cost[2] of counseling sessions; the particular role and responsibilities of client and counselor; and the focus of treatment.

The complex meanings of each of the various aspects of the contract need to be fully appreciated. What meaning does it have for the parishioner to meet for counseling in her minister's study? Will this be a place where she can feel safe? What will it be like for them to come to the minister's study in a small community, or to a large inner-city church at night? What about the contract as concerns confidentiality? The complexity of the contract needs to be appreciated, with opportunities for these complexities to be explored when counseling begins and when problems arise. It is the counselor's responsibility, as part of his or her training and expertise, to be sensitive to the dynamics around the contract, and help to make these explicit.

The initial contract that begins pastoral counseling, in which length, frequency, place, and cost of sessions are negotiated, will provide an opportunity to pay attention to power dynamics and relational boundaries. For example, once the length of sessions has been negotiated, then both the counselor and client can become aware of the subtle pulls toward disengagement, merger, overpowering and underpowering dynamics that may be evident when boundaries around the length of the session are bent or broken. When a client brings a gift or when personal information about the counselor is shared, then we cross over boundaries formed by the initial contract, some of which may have been made explicit, and some of which may have gone unstated. Gutheil and Gabbard note that "sexual misconduct usually begins with relatively minor boundary violations which often show a crescendo pattern of increasing intrusiveness into the patient's space which culminates in sexual contact" (Gutheil and Gabbard, 1993, 190). They are careful to point out that not all boundary crossings or even boundary violations lead to or represent evidence of sexual misconduct. For example, just because a counselor helps a client jump-start his car does not mean the counselor has started sliding down a slippery slope toward a sexual relationship! The initial contract that shapes the practical arrangements of care and counseling is helpful not in rigidly defining the boundaries, but rather in helping us monitor boundary crossings. One way to assess the malevolence or benevolence of such boundary crossings (like helping a client jump-start his car) is by considering power dynamics and relational boundaries. Does either crossing or not crossing a boundary create merged or disengaged dynamics? If, for example, I silently walk by my client whose car battery is dead, then is my maintenance of a boundary (not initiating conversation with a client outside of the consulting room) creating an inhumane form of disengagement? In this instance, assessing the relational boundaries created by my not crossing a boundary is important. Reflecting on the interaction of power dynamics and relational boundaries will happen intrapsychically within the counselor and collaboratively between counselor and client, and counselor and supervisor or consultant.

THE OUTSIDE CONTRACT

Of equal importance to the initial contract implicit in pastoral care and negotiated in pastoral counseling is the outside contract.[3] The outside contract involves the organizations to which the care giver or counselor is accountable: her or his congregation, her or his bishop, presbytery, or district superintendent, and the professional organization in which they are qualified as pastoral counselors; for example, the American Association of Pastoral Counselors or the American Association for Marriage and Family Therapists. The initial contractual negotiations between minister and parishioner or pastoral counselor and client are always negotiated within the context of these organizational structures.

For example, clergy need to be familiar with denominational guidelines on whether or not the pastoral care they provide needs to be supervised, and whether or not there are limits on the pastoral counseling contracts they make with parishioners. More and more denominations are suggesting or requiring that clergy only engage in crisis intervention with parishioners, that such intervention should not exceed three, four, or five sessions, and that clergy are obliged to make referrals if more pastoral counseling is needed. Such guidelines are being made more and more explicit in many denominations. These guidelines are part of the outside contract within which pastoral care and counseling occurs.

Another way of understanding the outside contract is through the standards of care that are defined for various professions and which become the basis for judging whether malpractice has occurred

(Denham and Denham, 1986, 84). In the past, lawsuits concerning clergy malpractice have used three sources for defining standards of conduct or care. The first source for defining the outside contract is the ordination vows and whatever standards for pastoral care and counseling are spelled out in one's particular denomination. For clergy who do pastoral counseling, the Code of Ethics of the American Association of Pastoral Counseling is used as the standard of care by which a minister's counseling is measured, regardless of whether the minister is a member of this organization. A second and third source for definitions of standards of conduct are community expectations regarding ministers and testimony from representatives of one's profession and denomination. In summary, the outside contract for pastoral care givers is shaped by the denomination to which they belong, and specifically their ordination vows and other statements concerning professional conduct. As well, there may be state laws that define particular aspects of pastoral care, such as the mandate to report elder or child abuse, or to protect suicidal parishioners or potential victims of homicidal parishioners. These laws vary from state to state, and are part of the outside contract that shapes pastoral care.

For pastoral counselors, the outside contract is much more de-tailed and specific than for pastoral care givers. This contract is spelled out in the ethical codes of professional associations like the American Association of Pastoral Counselors (AAPC), or the American Clinical Pastoral Educators (ACPE). As noted earlier, these codes have been used legally to define standards of care for pastoral care givers regardless of whether one is a member. The AAPC code of ethics forms the outside contract that exists between pastoral counselor and client and concerns foundational premises such as maintaining a responsible association with one's faith group, avoiding discrimina-tion, pursuing continuing education, engaging in collegial relation-ships, maintaining healthy personal lives, seeking assistance with personal problems, diagnosing and treating problems within our areas of competency, and establishing and maintaining appropriate boundaries in professional relationships (AAPC Code of Ethics, 1991). As well, the Code of Ethics outlines professional practices, client relationships, confidentiality, supervisee, student and em-ployee relationships, interprofessional relationships, and advertising. As such, this code forms a comprehensive outside contract to which all pastoral counselors and clergy who engage in pastoral counseling are accountable. When followed, the code becomes one important means for creating and monitoring appropriate relational boundaries and power dynamics.

THE TRANSFORMATION OF CONTRACT INTO COVENANT

The down-to-earth nature of both the initial contract (spelling out of frequency, duration, location, and cost of care or counseling) and the outside contract (spelling out of details of professional conduct) can be likened to the way in which a clay pot is prepared for the kiln. If the pot is carefully crafted, then it will be able to withstand the heat of the kiln. In the same way, if the initial contract is carefully crafted and the outside contract is meticulously adhered to, then the pastoral care or counseling relationship is less likely to break down and more likely to become a covenantal relationship.

Covenant is a rich and complex metaphor for a pastoral counseling or care relationship. It recalls the covenant made between God and God's people, and covenants made at important transitions in our lives: when our children are dedicated or baptized, when we are married, when we join a community of faith, or when we are ordained. The covenants we make with one another as human beings are continuous with and contained within the covenant made between God and us.

The essence of both the divine covenant and our human covenants is the promise to remain faithful to one another in the particular relationship we are entering: as parent, spouse, church member, and even minister or pastoral counselor. Remaining faithful involves monitoring the interaction of power dynamics and relational boundaries so that we don't move into overpowering, merged, or disengaged relationships. The promise implicitly made by parents toward children and by ministers toward parishioners is to assume responsibility for monitoring relational boundaries and power dynamics, given the structural power imbalance inherent in their roles as parents, ministers, and counselors. This recognizes that the relationship is not one between equals. The parent, minister, or counselor holds the balance of power and is responsible for maintaining the boundaries in the relationship, and getting help when the boundaries cannot be maintained.

When we can remain faithful to each other, the contracts we make at the outset of our relationships can become covenants: containers that heal, sustain, guide, and reconcile. Every empathic, empowering moment works toward creating covenantal containers.

CONCLUDING REMARKS

This book ends on a practical note, by talking about the initial and outside contracts of pastoral care and counseling and how such contracts can become covenants when we monitor the interaction of relational boundaries and power dynamics. The model of how power dynamics and relational boundaries interact is not intended as a sophisticated, high-powered, precise tool for navigation. It simply helps us get our bearings and reassures us that we are heading in the right direction. In a time when we are becoming more and more aware of the prevalence of abuse in our most trusted and sacred relationships, we need to once again know how to get our bearings; we need ways to monitor what is going on inside of us and what is happening in our families, congregations, and communities.

Within the past century, much of our pastoral care literature has talked about intrapsychic healing, and in the process has ignored the prevalence of violence in our families, communities, and culture. Looking back on this literature, we can see the extent to which this ignorance involved a collusion with those in power. When we lose sight of the prevalence of violence and are no longer monitoring dynamics related to violence, we contribute to violence and neglect. Perhaps we will not always need to constantly keep violence in sight if it becomes less prevalent and if every person, family, and community takes responsibility for monitoring power dynamics and relational boundaries. For now, in the contexts in which we practice as pastoral care givers and counselors, we must attend to the violence that is in our midst. This book is written in the hope that it will be a useful way to pay attention and in the process prevent abuse and neglect.

NOTES

INTRODUCTION

1. I published this prayer anonymously in a denominational newsletter written by women. It has since appeared in a variety of books (Gjerding and Kinnamon, 1983; Fortune, 1987, 59-61). Susan Thistlethwaite describes finding the poem "handwritten, taped to a bulletin board at the Cathedral of St. John the Divine in New York during the exhibit of Edwina Sandys's sculpture *Christa*" (Thistlethwaite, 1989, 162). I entitled the prayer, "By His Wounds You Have Been Healed" (1 Peter 2:24).

2. As I note in the fifth chapter, merger always implies an imbalance of power, with one substance swallowed up in the other. The more powerful substance remains intact, with the less powerful substance incorporated into it. Fusion involves the dissolution of boundaries between two equal substances, resulting in the formation of a new substance. I use the word *merger* throughout this book because of the ways in which power dynamics continually interact with relational boundaries to create merger and not fusion.

3. "Recognition is so central to human existence as to often escape notice; or, rather, it appears to us in so many guises that it is seldom grasped as one overarching concept. There are many near synonyms for it: to recognize is to affirm, validate, acknowledge, know, accept, understand, empathize, take in, tolerate, appreciate, see, identify with, find familiar, and love. What I call *mutual recognition* includes a number of experiences commonly described in the research on mother-infant interaction: emotional attunement, mutual influence, affective mutuality, and sharing states of mind" (Benjamin, 1988, 15-16).

4. "If the mother sets no limits for the child, if she obliterates herself and her own interests and allows herself to be wholly controlled, then she ceases to be a viable other for [the child] . . . If she retaliates, attempting to break his will, believing that any compromise will 'spoil' him, she will also inculcate the idea that there is room for only one ego in any relationship" (Benjamin, 1988, 39).

5. Jessica Benjamin (1988) notes that Freud, in highlighting the role of aggression in families, described domination using the metaphor of the father-son struggle. Benjamin uses feminist criticism and a reinterpretation of psychoanalytic theory to explore the problem of domination in terms of the subordination of women to men.

6. This chapter will be of particular interest to those who have been, like myself, deeply formed and transformed by art (for me, art became a means of sustenance and ultimately a way of experiencing who God was). For those who have simply enjoyed art, it may not seem so life-altering. For them, what I say in this chapter may seem overstated.

7. I have used texts like Flax (1990, 1993), Borgmann (1992), Brueggemann (1993), Ruf (1989), Smith (1990), and Taylor (1991) to better understand this cultural shift.

1. POWER DYNAMICS AND RELATIONAL BOUNDARIES IN CLERGY SEXUAL ABUSE

1. I will not attempt to replicate the novel's wit and humor, which tends to mask the degree of violence that lurks throughout its pages. In not highlighting the humor of the text and in focusing on its violence, I inevitably skew my reading of the novel. The intertwining of humor and violence is part of the complexity and paradox of this novel. Most readers focus on its humor; I will focus on its violence, acknowledging at the outset the limitations of this perspective.

2. The adjective *patriarchal* could be used to describe this American culture. Toril Moi cautions against viewing patriarchy as a conscious, unified conspiracy organized by men, saying that any "theory of sexual oppression as a conscious, monolithic plot against women leads to a seductively optimistic view of the possibilities for full liberation" (Moi, 1985, 29).

3. Because this is such a pervasive theme throughout the novel, it is tempting to limit our reading to this theme. We need to remind ourselves that this is a work of art which can be viewed from many angles.

4. "Sexual violation of trust is an epidemic, mainstream problem that reenacts in the professional relationship a wider cultural power imbalance between men and women" (Rutter, 1989, 2).

5. "There is something in *writing itself* which finally evades all systems and logics. There is a continual flickering, spilling and defusing of meaning" (Eagleton, 1983, 134).

6. Marshfield reminds me of a clergy sexual offender who continually sexualized his relationships with his female counselees by making "Freudian" interpretations to them. These interpretations were always highly sexual, and never about aggression. Of course, he made no interpretations of his counter-transference, either its sexual or aggressive dimensions.

7. Gordon Benson (1993, 149) notes, "sexual behavior in pastoral relationships is a topic that seems to evoke strongly polarized feelings, and often results in a polarized community." He goes on to describe unconscious countertransference reactions that contribute to polarization. When people "overidentify" with the "victim" there is a tendency to " 'overpathologize' the pastor, attributing all of his behavior to conscious attempts to control, manipulate, exploit or hurt. While in some cases the pastor may be antisocial or severely narcissistic, this is not always the case" (Benson, 1993, 150). This can lead to an "overinterpretation" of the pastor's behavior. Benson highlights here the need for a valuing of the unconscious dimensions of Marshfield's behavior, Updike's intentions, and the reader's response.

8. Rediger (1990, 15-17) has described these dynamics as the "star" factor that often is part of sexual acting out by male clergy. The external role of leading worship as though one were a performer in the spotlight may coincide with internal feelings of privilege, entitlement, and a heady sense of power over others. While Rediger doesn't spell out gender differences, one could infer that his descriptions fit male clergy more than female clergy, especially when he suggests that "the clergy role has always been sexually stimulating" and that a lack of external controls may tend to "loosen restrictions around genital expression" (Rediger, 1990, 16).

9. In a commentary which is somewhat sensitive to power dynamics, Ann-Janine Morey (1992b) describes how common it is in American novels about clergy in sexual relationships to highlight the adolescence of the clergy and the way women become "the necessary accomplices to and victims of his perpetual boyhood" (Morey, 1992b, 81). In *A Month of Sundays,* Marshfield's wife is cast in the role of distant, controlling mother, and Alicia becomes the indulgent mother and playmate.

10. A common theme that emerged from Gordon Benson's (1993, 119-126) interviews of male clergy involved in sexual misconduct was that these clergy had grandiose perceptions of their pastoral care, and they saw their sexual behavior as salvific for the women they counseled. While the theological theme of salvation ran throughout their life stories and stories of misconduct, there was a marked absence of sin as a theological theme.

11. Marie Fortune (1989, 110) notes that those who are betrayed by those who profess to represent God feel betrayed by God as well.

12. Benson (1993) found that all of the eight male clergy abusers he interviewed reported a lack of emotional intimacy in all of their significant relationships. For many this lack of intimacy was a lifelong experience. They described their fathers and mothers as distant. A prominent feature of the stories they told was their feelings of abandonment:

> Their experience was like being abandoned. Although they were provided with food, home, and shelter, they felt "alone" in the world. They often had similar feelings in adulthood. (Benson, 1993, 133)

13. As Ana-Marie Rizzuto (1979) and William Meissner (1984) suggest.
14. Schiff (1992, 22) suggests that the relationship between Marshfield and Prynne "represents, among other things, the writer's seduction and penetration of the reader." If so, it is a representation not simply of the sexual dimensions of this relationship between author and reader, but the dynamics of power imbalances, disengagement and merger that can happen between reader and author.
15. Peter Rutter writes that in such moments "nothing but sexual merger with the female body and spirit seems real" (Rutter, 1989, 5).
16. These diary entries depict the ways in which sex is used "in the service of narcissistic needs, such as narcissistic vulnerability, narcissistic injury, narcissistic swings from a deflated self to grandiosity" (Benson, 1993, 51). While Benson is describing a motivating factor in pastors who initiate sexual contact with female counselees, we see how the same factor may also be part of Marshfield's intense need for sexual contact with Ms. Prynne.
17. Many commentators see the sexual act between Marshfield and Prynne as a hopeful moment (Greiner, 1984; Uphaus, 1980), wherein Marshfield experiences true intimacy. For example, Schiff (1992, 50) writes, "Through his union with Ms. Prynne, Marshfield becomes whole again and is able to experience agape." Unlike the majority of critics, Detweiler (1984, 151) understands this as an "unsettling omen for his future."
18. Ann-Janine Morey (1992b) has taken up Updike's novel and reconsidered it in terms of some power dynamics, as I will highlight later in this chapter.
19. In what is called a post-structural literary perspective, one sees the novel or poem not "as a closed entity, equipped with definite meanings which it is the critic's task to decipher" but "as irreducibly plural, an endless play of signifiers which can never be finally nailed down to a single centre, essence or meaning" (Eagleton, 1983, 138).
20. Brueggemann (1993) describes how post-modernism—and with it the collapse of the world as we have known it—is frightening and can lead people to many kinds of brutality. The abuse of power can be understood as one instance of such brutality.
21. As, for example, in an article on male clergy adultery by Fishburn (1982). Many commentators explore the inter-relationship between this novel and Nathaniel Hawthorne's *Scarlet Letter,* made explicit in Updike's use of similar names like Prynne and Chillingworth (Greiner, 1984, 1985, 1989; Newman, 1988; Schiff, 1992), without commenting on the fact that both involve male clergy in sexually abusive relationships. A frequent statement about the inter-relationship of these novels is that they both describe the ambiguities and conflicts between sexual transgression and religion in American culture (Detweiler, 1979, 1984; Greiner, 1984, 1985; Hunt, 1980; Morey, 1992b). The most intricate textual analysis of this novel is done by Detweiler (1979), who undertakes a Lacanian structuralist reading. He describes this as a novel about the difficulty of communication. Blanche Gelfant's (1975) review, naming the abusive nature of the sexuality described in this novel, is labeled a tirade (Greiner, 1984).
22. Benson (1993, 43-46) notes that many current models classifying offending clergy do not adequately reflect the complexity of both the personality and behavior of offending clergy.
23. Rutter (1989, 5), in describing his own experience with an attractive client who offered herself to him sexually, wrote, "In the moment of deciding whether to cross this line, I felt all at once extremely powerful—and very, very vulnerable."
24. Rutter (1989) has described how therapists attempt to heal their own wounds through sexual contact with counselees. Philip has many wounds: his stigmatization, since birth, as

the child of unwed parents (notably a waitress and a student minister); the frustration of his vocation as an artist; the loss of an infant son; and the loss of an "adopted" twelve-year-old boy.

2. THE OVER-POWERING DISENGAGEMENT OF RACISM

1. Roberta Rubenstein highlights the role of relational boundaries when she says that "Toni Morrison's fiction . . . demonstrates a central interest in issues of boundary, attachment, and separation" (Rubenstein, 1993, 126).
2. I am indebted to a colleague, Linda Kirkland-Harris (1994), for her comments: "While it certainly appears that a disengaged, overpowering stance is operative in racism, the experience feels otherwise. There is an intricate and intimate involvement in active racism—the maintenance of structure and processes of oppression require constant involvement with one's notion of the other, if not with the physical reality of the other. It's more merged than disengaged. The projection and displacement involved in prejudice perhaps account for the appearance of disengagement. But racism, from my perspective, signifies distortion of ontological proportions."
3. Holloway (1992) comments that generally speaking, female African American authors write about violence in an empathic way, unlike male writers where "evil is an omnipresent, earth-bound presence" depicted with a "series of graphic and violent moments" in which the reader may simply feel overwhelmed and immersed in the violence (Holloway, 1992, 9).
4. Valerie Smith (1993, 345-355) notes the focus throughout *Beloved* on the human bodies of its characters. She draws upon an idea that is central in Elaine Scarry's (1985) book *The Body in Pain*: no matter how vividly we use language to describe physical pain, it remains inexpressible. Morrison's focus on the human body is an attempt to depict the extreme pain inflicted on African Americans. Besides depicting pain, Morrison is also attempting to depict the experience of mothers and infants being separated from one another. Sensory communication is the primary mode of expression between a parent and infant. When there is a separation, then yearning for connection can take the primary form of yearning for the sensuous experience of the other.
5. Margaret Atwood comments that the slavery Morrison depicts is "one of the most viciously anti-family institutions human beings have ever devised. The slaves are motherless, fatherless, deprived of their mates, their children, their kin" (Atwood, 1993, 34).
6. Trudier Harris (1993, 330) describes Stamp Paid as someone who was owned during slavery but was never possessed, in that he remained empathic and empowered and didn't become overpowered by the external realities of slavery.
7. Linda Kirkland-Harris (1994) notes: "One way in which black people talk about their experience of white people as the social embodiment and driving force of racism is that there is something fundamentally different and incomprehensible about them. This something is manifested in the repeated will to be genocidal as a means of material gain; hatred of people of color; and incapacity to conceive of others' well-being as compatible with rather than an express threat to their own."
8. She notes that artists "transferred internal conflicts to a 'blank darkness', to conveniently bound and violently silenced black bodies" and that this is a major theme in American literature (Morrison, 1992, 38).
9. Morrison draws the reader into this intrapsychic process by only giving us fragments of memories.
10. Morrison, like her character Paul, "writes to awaken her reader's sensitivity, to wake up and disrupt the sensual numbing that accompanies social and psychological alienation" (Willis, 1993, 323).
11. "In carving out a definition of motherhood in a world where she had no models for that status [of motherhood] . . . Sethe has erred on the side of excess, a destructive excess that inadvertently gives primacy to the past and death rather than to life and the future" (Trudier Harris, 1993, 339).

12. Morrison (Rothstein, 1987), in discussing the writing of *Beloved,* noted that she was describing a mother-love that becomes deadly when a mother suppresses or displaces her own self in the process of mothering. This disengagement from herself, when accompanied by a merger within the world of the child is a "killer" form of mother-love.

13. This three-part movement, from being exposed to brutality, to invoking the name of Jesus, and then to transformative action, is described in many texts on practical theology. For example, Browning (1991) describes practical theology as (1) beginning with a thick description in which one apprehends the complexity of the experience, then (2) moving to normative biblical and theological texts (similar to the invoking of Jesus' name) and finally (3) working toward a transformation rooted in one's theology.

14. Susan Thistlethwaite (1989) has used African American women's fiction to reflect upon the differences that class and race make in feminist theology.

15. "The result has been an astonishing intellectual effort, channelled into politics-as-judicial-review, that has made law schools the dynamic centres of social and political thought on American campuses; and also a series of titanic battles over what used to be the relatively routine . . . matter of senatorial confirmation of presidential appointments to the Supreme Court" (Taylor, 1991, 115).

16. We need to beware of a form of individualism based on the idea that each human being has a unique potential: "this idea entered very deeply into modern consciousness. . . . Before the late eighteenth century no one thought that the differences between human beings had this kind of moral significance. . . . This is the powerful moral ideal that has come down to us" (Taylor, 1991, 28-29).

3. LIFE-GIVING SEXUAL AND SPIRITUAL DESIRE

1. Lindsey Tucker (1992, 7) describes Murdoch's characters thus: "While it can . . . be argued that her gallery of characters comes from only the professional classes, the literary and the artistic, this seemingly narrow social range belies an assortment of individuals—a plethora of waifs, refugees, magicians, mystics, and demonic personalities . . ."

2. I wonder whether a revelation or positive sign would be overpowering, submerging Anne in God. The negative and agnostic sign is, in fact, empowering, as long as Anne is attuned to God, and not disengaged from God.

3. "In the hands of a less skillful novelist, a vision of Christ received by an ex-nun would be somehow tied to orthodoxy and send Anne running back to the community of the convent and the bosom of the Church, but the intelligent agnosticism with which it is treated here is complex and pointed" (Dipple, 1982, 327).

4. Dipple (1982, 328) notes that their conversation contains almost direct quotations from Julian Norwich's *Revelations of Divine Love.*

5. "Although this Christ may be simply a vision, his searing reality scars Anne permanently beyond the aid of antibiotics, and his cosmic manifestations haunt the background of the novel" (Dipple, 1982, 308).

6. Dipple (1982, 310) described this as an instance of Anne using "the concept of God without theory or fantasy."

7. Dipple says that the other two "elements" rejected in this novel are God and philosophy (especially Wittgenstein), which are also depicted as "powerful, even overpowering forces" (Dipple, 1982, 310).

4. POWER DYNAMICS IN PASTORAL CARE AND COUNSELING

1. Guggenbuhl-Craig, 1971, iii.

2. "The problem is that influential theories, rooted within the systemic paradigm, have obscured the context of family interaction and the operation of power within families and the larger system" (Fish, 1993, 227). Fish also critiques contemporary approaches in

169

marriage and family therapy which focus on family narratives, saying that they unwittingly "enforce a conceptual blackout [of socio-political context and power] which begins at the edges of the family's story or conversation" (Fish, 1993, 228).

3. I wonder whether there is some connection between the focus on families and self-determination during the 1950s and the witnessing of—and to some extent identification with—husbands separated from wives and parents separated from children in the midst of violence when the bombs were dropped on Hiroshima and Nagasaki, and when Jewish people were attacked, transported, encamped, and exterminated during the Second World War. One has only to glimpse these separations once and one is haunted by them forever.

4. Jessica Benjamin (1988) uses the terms *self-assertion* and *mutual recognition* to describe empowering relationships that are mutually respectful. In her descriptions of the need for both assertion and recognition, she may be alluding to the ways in which power (assertion) and relational boundaries (mutual recognition) may interact to form life-giving relationships.

5. Also highlighted was my need for consultation and supervision. Compared with my actual supervisor, my "inner" supervisor was demanding and harsh.

6. As Guggenbuhl-Craig (1971, 85) comments: "In a human relationship one subject confronts another. Each relates to the other as subject. In a relationship in which power is a dominant factor, one subject tries to make an object out of the other."

7. We can see how this process also involves relational boundaries: "Doctor[s] may turn [patients] into an object of [their] power drive. . . . [They] objectif[y] illness, distance [themselves] from [their] own weakness, elevate [themselves] and degrade the patient" (Guggenbuhl-Craig, 1971, 94). This is an overpowering, disengaged relationship.

8. Bohler (1994) explores this in her discussion of subjectivity.

9. Marie Fortune (1983) does this in creating two continua, one for consensual sexuality (with receptive and proactive poles) and one for coercive sexuality. While such a distinction is helpful in dispelling the myth that rape is sex that "got out of hand," it may also help us ignore unsettling power dynamics that are present in sexual relationships.

10. Chris Schlauch (*Faithful Companioning*, forthcoming) has called this quality of relationship in pastoral psychotherapy faithful companioning.

11. Judith Herman (1992) describes the extent to which the personality and coping skills are altered by long-term exposure to abuse in a totalitarian context. Jessica Benjamin (1988) uses psychoanalytic and feminist theories to explore the intrapsychic ways in which women get caught in the role of the dominated.

12. For an excellent presentation of a systems perspective of power imbalances, see Graham (1992).

13. In a review of eight professional codes of conduct from diverse helping professions, Lebacqz highlights how the professional's expertise is only one of fifteen items that define one's professional role (Lebacqz, 1985, 69).

14. For a discussion of how stereotypes of African American women as mammies, matriarchs, welfare recipients, and hot mommas have been part of racism, see Collins (1991).

15. Augsburger, 1986; Hinkle and Hinkle, 1992; Karaban, 1991; McCarthy, 1992.

16. The inter-relationship between the terms *post-structural* and *post-modern* is complex. I understand *post-structural* to refer to a philosophical stance that questions the inherent meanings we ascribe to reality and deconstructs these meanings. I use the term *post-modern* to describe the ways in which Western culture no longer is oriented toward the individual and no longer understands the scientific method as the only means of accumulating more and more pieces of the puzzle we used to call reality.

17. Ruf (1989, 31-32) describes this deep structure as "a supreme principle (a logos) knowable to us that organizes all of these differences into a system of necessary relationships."

18. "The end of modernity requires a critique of method in scripture study. . . . Conventional historical criticism is, in scripture study, our particular practice of modernity, whereby the text was made to fit our modes of knowledge and control" (Brueggemann, 1993, 11).

19. "Deconstruction's moral and political import seems to be primarily critical in character. Deconstruction serves the purposes of criticism, the criticism of the totalitarianism of modern regimes" (Walsh, 1989, 124).

20. A strict Derridean stance does not seem to allow for this "in-between," since its aim is to de-contaminate a philosophy polluted by Western metaphysics and ontotheology. Hence, living in the flux would inevitably be contaminated by some sense of ultimate meaning or presence.

21. "We long for knowable origins that connect to guaranteed ends (including the goodness of our purposes and agency) and for a loving home. We wish for a meaningful, purposive, orderly, continuous, stable, nurturing, friendly and comprehensible universe, and for secure roots" (Flax, 1993, 71).

5. RELATIONAL BOUNDARIES IN PASTORAL CARE AND COUNSELING

1. Winnicott (1960, 34), in an essay entitled "The Capacity to be Alone," uses the term *disengagement* to describe "being alone in the presence of the other," a way of being with others in which one recognizes the other, but does not feel compelled to interact. As I use the term *disengagement* it involves detachment without recognition of the other's humanity.

2. Hartmann describes sixteen different types of boundaries (1991, 22-23). In describing the differences between those who are disengaged and those who are merged, I find five of these types of boundaries helpful: (1) boundaries separating thoughts and feelings; (2) interpersonal boundaries; (3) boundaries between conscious and unconscious; (4) boundaries related to identity (sexual identity, age identity and constancy of identity); and (5) boundaries as defense mechanisms.

3. A difficulty with using Chodorow's thesis is that the complex strands of development taking place during the first years can be too easily reduced to this single strand: boys differentiating their anatomy from that of their mothers and girls having difficulty establishing a sense of being different (and at the same time enjoying an ongoing sense of connection with their mothers because of their common sex). For a detailed description of how a need for self-assertion (what I identify as empowerment) and mutual recognition (what I identify as empathy) interact in early childhood and how this shapes gender, see Jessica Benjamin (1988). For how a psychodynamic understanding of gender development can inform pastoral care, see Maxine Glaz and Jeanne Stevenson Moessner (1991).

4. This is Heinz Kohut's definition. For a synopsis of a psychodynamic understanding of empathy and an understanding of empathy as the essence of pastoral psychotherapy, see Schlauch (1990).

5. I have considered this more fully elsewhere (Doehring, 1993a).

6. As Jessica Benjamin (1988) notes.

6. THE INTERACTION OF POWER DYNAMICS AND RELATIONAL BOUNDARIES IN OUR RELATIONSHIP WITH GOD

1. Jessica Benjamin (1988) describes the interacting dynamics of self-assertion and mutual recognition as life-giving.

2. This passion for connection involves "tak[ing] our body experiences seriously as occasions for revelation" (James Nelson, 1992, 9). In order to do this, we cannot be disengaged from our sexual desires, nor submerged in them. Those who argue that sexual desire has nothing to do with spiritual desire create a dualism of body and spirit. Some sort of disengagement and devaluing results: disengagement from and devaluing of either our spiritual desire or our sexual desire.

3. Sometimes when people try to identify formative or transformative events, no particular memory stands out. It may be helpful for people to identify ongoing processes that were either formative or transformative. It may be particularly difficult to identify life-giving formative events or processes because, to use an analogy, they are like food that gets taken in and becomes part of the cells, blood, and bones of the body. Life-giving events may become built into the personality structure without one's awareness. Destructive events or

171

processes may stand out more, unless they have been consciously repressed. Eagle proposes that maladaptive and pathogenic relationships are internalized in a different way from life-giving relationships: "In bad experiences, the bad object [the maladaptive relationship] is internalized as object, undigested and unassimilated, and hence remains as a foreign body within the psychic structure of the individual" (Eagle, 1983, 78).

4. When we consider anything that mediates connection with someone not physically present as a transitional object, then we can appreciate the ways in which religious signs, symbols, and sacraments may function as transitional objects. Our religious signs, symbols, and sacraments convey the reality of God.

5. Meissner describes the tensions of interfacing psychoanalytic and religious thinking, each with "its own discourse, reference points, and modes of conceptualization and symbolic connotation" (Meissner, 1992, 185). He characterizes religious thinking as asserting "unequivocally that there is a God" (Meissner, 1992, 185) and psychoanalytic thinking as being wholly concerned with the inner world of psychic experience. Such a characterization omits both the religious thinking that questions who God is, and the psychoanalytic thinking that interfaces external interpersonal and social realities with intrapsychic realities. Meissner suggests that Winnicott's concept of transitional phenomena, describing an area of illusion that is neither subjective nor objective, can be a useful bridging model between psychoanalytic and religious discourse.

6. For an elaboration of this model and the way we can understand the impact of child abuse on women's adult images of God, see Doehring (1993b).

7. Research on the role of fundamentalist religious systems in the etiology of multiple personality disorders suggests that when fundamentalist Christianity and strict religious practices are combined with severe punishments and emotional or sexual repression, the only way for some children to cope is to disassociate and create impenetrable walls between opposing constellations of God, self, and parent representations (Gottlieb, 1977; Saltman and Solomon, 1982). Coons (1980) found that among multiple personality clients who found religion important, one personality frequently espoused a fundamentalist religion, while another personality was atheistic or rebelled against religion.

8. The sample was limited in that it was drawn from graduate degree programs in social work, theology, and psychology.

9. Many friends have described opposite experiences of the nuns in their schools. For them they represented a safe, stable environment.

10. Moshe Spero (1992) describes the work of pastoral counseling as a process of folding back the layers and layers of projected God representations, so that we can slowly experience the fullness of God's being.

11. Fish-Murray, Koby, and van der Kolk's study (1987) comparing severely abused children with non-abused children found that severely abused children showed inflexibility in cognitive schemata and had markedly different concepts of justice in which rules were made and infractions punished by the largest male. We can hear an implicit image of an overpowering, punishing male God in this concept.

12. Bradford (1990, 38), in a study comparing the psychologies of early Christian martyrs with individual cases involving borderline personality disorders, suicide, and self-mutilation, notes that "distinctions between normal and abnormal religiousness are not easily made. . . . Distinguishing normal from abnormal religiousness may require analysis of such psychologically subtle matters as phenomenology of body image."

13. Jessica Benjamin (1988) describes fears of abandonment as arising from both experiences of parents being absent and experiences of parents drawing children into merger.

14. This is a problem with Carter Heyward's argument in her book *When Boundaries Betray Us*. Heyward describes her experience of being in a therapeutic relationship that kindled a profound transference. She wanted to renegotiate the relationship to include a friendship. For Heyward, her overpowering desire for connection made it difficult for her to recognize the necessity for separation, specifically the separations protected by the therapeutic contract. She experienced these boundaries as creating disengagement and a power differential which felt not only too painful to bear but theologically wrong.

15. Such disengagement is depicted in Shirley Jackson's 1950s short story "The Lottery." In this short story, once the victim is selected, the community sees her no longer as one of their own, but simply as an object that must be destroyed.

16. "Jesus Christ the Apple Tree" in Holbrook, David and Elizabeth Poston. *The Cambridge Hymnal*. (Cambridge: Cambridge University Press, 1967), 168-69.

17. "When for Eternal Worlds We Steer" in *Sixty Hymns from the Songs of Zion*. (Whittier, California: Praise Publications, 1977), 53.

18. " 'Negative theology' has come to designate a certain typical attitude toward language. . . . Suppose, by a provisional hypothesis, that negative theology consists of considering that every predicative language is inadequate to the essence, in truth to the hyperessentiality (the Being beyond being) of God; consequently, only a negative ('apophatic') attribution can claim to approach God, and to prepare us for a silent intuition of God" (Derrida, 1992, 74).

19. Morny Joy (1992, 263) characterizes Derrida as standing on the threshold, an exile, an outsider, "the wandering Reb Derrida to all Greek and Christian ontological homecomings."

20. Grotstein (1991, 16) comments that "self-regulatory deficits, in other words, partake of the power/powerlessness dialect."

21. Grotstein likens this kind of "backing" with the comfort a child receives from sitting in a caretaker's lap.

22. Grotstein's development of his ideas is quite complex and includes the systems perspective that the infant-parent relationship is interactive: "the infant regulates its mother [/father], as well as the reverse" (Grotstein, 1991, 7).

7. UNDERSTANDING SIN
AS DISENGAGEMENT, MERGER, AND POWER IMBALANCES

1. See Carter Heyward (1989) and Rita Nakashima Brock (1991).

2. Another text, Roger Scruton's book *Sexual Desire: A Moral Philosophy of the Erotic* (1986) reviews all of the philosophical writings on sexual desire, and argues that life-giving sexual desire must be interpersonal (that is, within a relationship that values the other).

3. Benjamin (1988) uses the *Story of O* to illustrate a sexual enslavement in particular, and women's subordination by men in general. As was noted with Anne Marie Hunter's use of the experience of male batterers stalking female partners and ex-partners (in the previous chapter), it is problematic to generalize from the experience of some women (e.g., the woman in the *Story of O,* and women stalked by partners or ex-partners) to all women. A second problem with Benjamin's illustration is that she remains focused on the erotic master-slave relationship to the exclusion of other forms of master-slave relationships, for example, those of Euro-American masters and African American slaves.

4. It is complex to distinguish between disengagement and merger when it comes to abusive dynamics. It can be helpful to think of disengagement as coldness, a "not wanting to know anything about the other" combined with objectifying the other and using them. This can be contrasted with merger, which is like a smothering hothouse and may involve an invasive quality of "wanting to know everything about the other." The two dynamics can be combined, where there is a cold invasive cruelty toward another.

5. "The idea of mutual recognition seems to me an ever more crucial category of early experience. Increasingly, research reveals infants to be active participants who help shape the responses of their environment and "create" their own objects. Through its focus on interaction, infancy research has gradually widened psychology's angle of observation to include infant *and* parent, the simultaneous presence of two living subjects" (Benjamin, 1988, 16). Benjamin goes on to note that "the mother as a subject in her own right" has only just been acknowledged and that "no psychological theory has adequately articulated the mother's independent existence" (Benjamin, 1988, 23).

6. Chodorow (1978) objects to this, saying that Dinnerstein does not distinguish between infantile fantasies about maternal power and the actual power that mothers have.
7. Gordon Benson (1993) found the theological theme of salvation—and specifically salvific healing through sex—recurring through his interviews with clergy who had been sexually involved with female counselees. The theological theme of sin was notably absent.
8. "There is a wealth of clinical evidence to suggest that, in this culture, genital sexual activity is a prominent feature in the maintenance of masculine gender while it is a variable feature in feminine gender. . . . In men, gender appears to 'lean' on sexuality. . . . In women, gender identity and self-worth can be consolidated by other means" (Person, 1980, 619).
9. The use of the word *external* may oversimplify the distinction between external and internal. An external reality in which one is actually overpowered may become internalized. As an internal reality it may continue to function in settings where one is not overpowered.
10. His sexual escapades as a window washer may be his way of reclaiming some kind of power.
11. A particular difficulty with naming one's sexual desires is that such desires are idiosyncratic. Ethel Person (1980) uses the term *sex print* (like a fingerprint) to describe the highly idiosyncratic configurations of sexual attraction which are shaped by internal representations.
12. Benson (1993) noted all of the clergy involved in sexual misconduct that he interviewed reported a lack of emotional intimacy in adulthood, and for many of these men, in childhood.

8. USING LITERATURE AS CASE STUDIES

1. Reader-oriented theories of literary criticism look at what fiction evokes in the reader. For a summary of these approaches, see Selden and Widdowson (1993).
2. "The escape that fiction provides is an escape from social responsibility, a flight sometimes necessary for emotional equilibrium, but at other times a replacement for genuine participation" (Detweiler, 1989, 32).
3. Giles Gunn (1979, 176-77) uses similar language in describing "our characteristic inability through an act of imagination to get outside of our own skins." His evidence for this "inability to see, much less feel, other people as real human beings" is the massive injustices suffered by African American, Native American, and Mexican American people. He goes on to note how some American writers have "proposed as an antidote, not the need for an imaginative, sympathetic fathoming of individual differences, but rather some illusory fantasy of engrossment with or complete submergence in the life of the 'other' " (Gunn, 1979, 178).
4. Morrison (1992, 5) notes the paradoxical way in which the absence of overt references to Black people or images may actually involve the pervasive, unnamed presence of "a dark, abiding, singing Africanist presence."
5. Murdoch's pessimism is rooted in her classically Freudian perspective. Don Browning argues that Freud had a cautious and limited view of humanity, shaped by humanity's "limited libidinal investments or . . . ready hostilities." He characterizes Freud's culture as one of civilized detachment. "The culture of detachment sees the world as basically hostile and humans as largely self-absorbed creatures with only small amounts of energy for larger altruistic ventures" (Browning 1987, 5).
6. According to Giles Gunn (1979, 120), literature always mediates "a form of otherness, a sense of things not quite our own." Gunn goes on to describe the new self-knowledge we appropriate through the "otherness" of the novel: "Ricoeur speaks of this process as appropriation. Appropriation in this sense is far removed from its usual meaning 'as a way of taking hold of things,' of possessing them [we might note the power dynamics being described here]; instead it represents a kind of dispossession in which the new modes of being projected by the work in turn afford the reader with new possibilities of self knowledge" (Gunn, 1979, 121).
7. Gunn is quoting from D. H. Lawrence (1951).

8. A contemporary difficulty with looking at the interface between theology and literary criticism is the sheer multitude of models and theories that now exist under each of these disciplines. For example, an introductory text on literary theory such as Selden and Widdowson's (1993) ranges over the following literary theories: new criticism, moral formalism and F. R. Leavis, Russian formalism, reader-oriented theory, Marxist theories, structuralist theories, poststructuralist theories, post-modern and postcolonialist theories, and feminist theories. An overview of current theological models would have the same diversity. When one considers all the possible combinations of literary critical models and theological models, there are many possible interdisciplinary models one could develop.

The most recent review articles of the interdisciplinary study of literature and theology highlight the new horizons opened up by post-structuralist theory (Kort, 1990; Morey, 1992a). The horizons are so expansive that some have questioned whether there is anything left of this interdisciplinary study. If the interdisciplinary study of literature and theology arose in a modernist matrix, as some have supposed (Kort, 1990), can it survive in a post-modern context? If one no longer operates with assumptions that literature bespeaks "transhistorical and authoritative realities" (Kort, 1990, 575) then is any conversation possible between literature and theology? If one looks beyond the horizons of meaning created by modernism, one can see many directions in which to go. While no single direction can offer the "true" interdisciplinary study of literature and theology, it is possible to try different combinations of literary critical and theological models and create lively interdisciplinary conversations.

9. Gunn (1979) describes four predominant approaches to literature: mimetic (where litera-ture is not so much simply a mirror of reality, but a lens through which to see "what is essential or basic about reality" [Gunn, 1979, 59]); pragmatic (literature is less an imitation and more an invention for pragmatic purposes—chiefly moral ones); Romantic (literature is an expression of "the assimilating power of the creative imagination" [Gunn, 1979, 62]); the modern, semantic, formalist approach (literature has a particular language and par-ticular forms of expression that can be viewed objectively and technically, without reference to the artist, the audience or the world it describes).

Gunn (1979, 58) notes that the mimetic approach focuses on "the world the work creates and reveals"; the pragmatic approach focuses on "the audience the work affects"; the Romantic approach focuses on "the artist who creates the work"; and the formalist approach focuses on the work itself.

10. I am borrowing this image from Gunn (1979, 35).

11. "When a position is really comfortable—wonderfully defended from within and reinforced by culture—we do not experience it as a position, just as introspection may not tell fish about water or people about air. . . . We swim in other unfelt seas: xenophobias, racisms, sexisms. Who knows what next will bring us up gasping" (Stoller, 1991, 1097).

9. MONITORING RELATIONAL BOUNDARIES AND POWER DYNAMICS IN PASTORAL CARE AND COUNSELING

1. Clebsch and Jaekle (1964) have described these as four functions that have characterized the way pastoral care has been practiced throughout Christianity.

2. By cost I do not simply mean financial fees. Counseling involves an investment of time and energy for everyone involved. When a minister and couple agree to meet three times to talk about a marital crisis, they are each giving time and energy to the counseling sessions.

3. Rice and Rutan (1987, 83), writing about group psychotherapy in an institutional setting, use the term *outside contract* to describe the agreement with the administration as to what the goals for group therapy will be and how the group will be organized.

BIBLIOGRAPHY

Amis, Martin. "Blown Away." *The New Yorker,* May 30, 1994, 47-49.

Arnold, David Scott. *Liminal Readings: Forms of Otherness in Melville, Joyce and Murdoch.* New York: St. Martin's Press, 1993.

Atwood, Margaret. *The Edible Woman.* Toronto: McClelland and Stewart, 1969.

_____. Review of *Beloved,* by Toni Morrison. *The New York Times Book Review,* September 13, 1987.

Augsburger, David. *Pastoral Counseling Across Cultures.* Philadelphia: Westminster Press, 1986.

Benjamin, Jessica. *The Bonds of Love: Psychoanalysis, Feminism, and the Problem of Domination.* New York: Pantheon Books, 1988.

Benson, Gordon. "Sexual Misconduct by Male Clergy with Adult Female Counselees: Systematic and Situational Themes." Ph.D. diss., Boston University, 1993.

Beres, D., and E. Joseph, "The Concept of Mental Representation in Psychoanalysis." *International Journal of Psychoanalysis* 51 (1970): 1-9.

Blake, William. Quoted in David Holbrook and Elizabeth Poston. *The Cambridge Hymnal.* Cambridge: Cambridge University Press, 1967.

Bohler, Carolyn. "Subjectively Speaking." *Journal of Pastoral Theology* 4 (1994): 32-48.

Borgmann, Albert. *Crossing the Post-Modern Divide.* Chicago: The University of Chicago Press, 1992.

Bradford, D. T. "Early Christian Martyrdom and the Psychology of Depression, Suicide and Bodily Mutilation." *Psychotherapy* 27 (1990): 30-41.

Brock, Rita Nakashima. *Journeys by Heart: A Christology of Erotic Power.* New York: Crossroad, 1991.

Brown, Joanne, and Carole Bohn, eds. *Christianity, Patriarchy and Abuse: A Feminist Critique.* New York: The Pilgrim Press, 1989.

Browning, Don S. *A Fundamental Practical Theology: Descriptive and Strategic Proposals.* Minneapolis: Fortress Press, 1991.

_____. *Religious Thought and the Modern Psychologies: A Critical Conversation in the Theology of Culture.* Philadelphia: Fortress, 1987.

Brueggemann, Walter. *Texts Under Negotiation: The Bible and Postmodern Imagination.* Philadelphia: Fortress, 1993.

Caldwell, Gail. "Morrison Awarded Nobel." *The Boston Globe,* October 8, 1993, 1, 16.

Cannon, Katie. *Black Womanist Ethics.* Atlanta: Scholars Press, 1988.

_____. "Resources for a Constructive Ethic in the Life and Work of Zora Neale Hurston." *Journal of Feminist Studies in Religion* 1:1 (1985): 37-51.

Caputo, John. *Radical Hermeneutics: Repetition, Deconstruction and the Hermeneutic Protest.* Bloomington: Indiana University Press, 1987.

Carver, Raymond. *Where I'm Calling from: New and Selected Stories.* New York: Atlantic Monthly Press, 1988.

Chodorow, Nancy. *The Reproduction of Mothering: Psychoanalysis and the Sociology of Gender.* Berkeley: University of California, 1978.

Clebsch, William A., and Charles, R. Jaekle. *Pastoral Care in Historical Perspective: An Essay With Exhibits.* Englewood Cliffs, N. J.: Prentice-Hall, 1964.

Collins, Patricia Hill. *Black Feminist Thought: Knowledge, Consciousness, and the Politics of Empowerment.* New York: Routledge, 1991.

Coons, P. M. "Multiple Personality: Diagnostic Considerations." *Journal of Clinical Psychiatry* 41 (1980): 330-36.

Couture, Pamela. *Blessed Are the Poor? Women's Poverty, Family Policy, and Practical Theology.* Nashville: Abingdon Press, 1991.

Cushman, Philip. "Ideology Obscured: Political Uses of the Self in Daniel Stern's Baby." *American Psychologist* March (1991): 206-19.

Datan, Nancy. "Aging into Transitions: Cross-cultural Perspectives on Women at Midlife." In Ruth Formanek, ed. *The Meanings of Menopause: Historical, Medical and Clinical Perspectives.* Hillsdale, N.J.: The Analytic Press, 1990.

Denham, Thomas E., and Melinda Denham. "Avoiding Malpractice Suits in Pastoral Counseling." *Pastoral Psychology* 35 (1986): 83-93.

Derrida, Jacques. "How to Avoid Speaking: Denials." Translated by Ken Frieden in Harold Coward and Toby Foshay, eds. *Derrida and Negative Theology.* Albany: State University of New York Press, 1992. Reprinted from Sanford Budick and Wolfgang Iser. *Languages of the Unsayable: The Play of Negativity in Literature and Literary Theory.* New York: Columbia University Press, 1989.

177

Despland, Michel. "On Not Solving Riddles Alone." In Harold Coward and Toby Foshay, eds. *Derrida and Negative Theology.* Albany: State University of New York Press, 1992.

Detweiler, Robert. *Breaking the Fall: Religious Readings of Contemporary Fiction.* San Francisco: Harper & Row, 1989.

_____. *Four Spiritual Crises in Mid-Century American Fiction.* Gainesville: University of Florida Press, 1963.

_____. *John Updike.* Rev. ed. Boston: Twayne Publishers, 1984.

_____. "Updike's *A Month of Sundays* and the Language of the Unconscious." *Journal of the American Academy of Religion* 47 (1979): 609-25.

Dinnerstein, Dorothy. *The Mermaid and the Minotaur: Sexual Arrangements and Human Malaise.* New York: Harper & Row, 1976.

Dipple, Elizabeth. *Iris Murdoch: Work of the Spirit.* Chicago: University of Chicago Press, 1982.

Doehring, Carrie. "The Absent God: When Neglect Follows Sexual Violence." *The Journal of Pastoral Care* 47 (1993 a): 3-12.

_____. "Developing Models of Feminist Pastoral Counseling." *The Journal of Pastoral Care* 46 (1992): 23-32.

_____. *Internal Desecration: Traumatization and God Representations.* Lanham, Md.: University Press of America, 1993b.

_____. "Life-giving Sexual and Spiritual Desire." *Journal of Pastoral Theology* 4 (1994): 49-69.

Eagle, M. N. *Recent Developments in Psychoanalysis: A Critical Evaluation.* New York: McGraw-Hill, 1984.

Eagleton, Terry. *Literary Theory: An Introduction.* Minneapolis: University of Minnesota Press, 1983.

Edwards, Jonathan. "Sinners in the Hands of an Angry God." In Richard Poirier and William Vance, eds. *American Literature: Volume 1.* Boston: Little, Brown and Company, 1970.

Ellis, Bret Easton. *American Psycho: A Novel.* New York: Vintage Books, 1991.

_____. *Less Than Zero.* New York: Penguin Books, 1987.

Evans, James H., Jr. *Spiritual Empowerment in Afro-American Literature.* The Edwin Mellen Press, 1987.

_____. "African-American Christianity and the Post-modern Condition." *Journal of the American Academy of Religion* 43:2 (1990): 207-22.

Fernando, Suman. *Race and Culture in Psychiatry.* London: Routledge, 1989.

Fish, Vincent. "Poststructuralism in Family Therapy: Interrogating the Narrative/Conversational Mode." *Journal of Marital and Family Therapy* 19 (1993): 221-32.

Fish-Murray, C. G., E. V. Koby, and B. A. van der Kolk. "Evolving Ideas: The Effects of Abuse on Children's Thought." In B. A. van der Kolk, ed. *Psychological Trauma.* Washington, D. C.: American Psychiatric Press, 1987.

Fishburn, Janet. "Male Clergy Adultery as Vocational Confusion." *The Christian Century*, Sept. 15-22 (1982): 922-25.

Flax, Jane. *Disputed Subjects: Essays on Psychoanalysis, Politics, and Philosophy.* New York: Routledge, 1993.

_____. *Thinking Fragments: Psychoanalysis, Feminism, and Postmodernism in the Contemporary West.* Berkeley: University of California Press, 1990.

Flinn, Frank K. "Reconstructing the Deconstruction of Ontology." In Henry Ruf, ed. *Religion, Ontotheology and Deconstruction.* New York: Paragon House, 1989.

Fortune, Marie. *Is Nothing Sacred? When Sex Invades the Pastoral Relationship.* San Francisco: Harper & Row, 1989.

_____. *Keeping the Faith: Questions and Answers for the Abused Woman.* San Francisco: Harper & Row, 1987.

_____. *Sexual Violence: The Unmentionable Sin.* New York: Pilgrim Press, 1983.

Gallop, Jane. "Reading the Mother Tongue: Psychoanalytic Feminist Criticism." In Francoise Meltzer, ed. *The Trials of Psychoanalysis.* Chicago: The University of Chicago Press, 1987.

Gelfant, Blanche. "Fiction Chronicle." *Hudson Review* 28 (1975).

Gerkin, Charles V. *Prophetic Pastoral Practice: A Christian Vision of Life Together.* Nashville: Abingdon Press, 1991.

Gilligan, Carol. *In a Different Voice: Psychological Theory and Women's Development.* Cambridge: Harvard University Press, 1982.

Girard, Renée. *Things Hidden Since the Foundation of the World.* Translated by S. Bann and M. Metteer. Stanford: Stanford University Press, 1987.

Gjerding, Iben, and Katherine Kinnamon. *No Longer Strangers: A Resource for Women and Worship.* Geneva: World Council of Churches, 1983.

Glaz, Maxine, and Jeanne Stevenson Moessner, eds. *Women in Travail and Transition: A New Pastoral Care.* Minneapolis: Fortress Press, 1991.

Gottlieb, J. "Multiple Personality: A Continuing Enigma." *Current Concepts in Psychiatry* January-February (1977): 15-23.

Graham, Larry Kent. *Care of Person, Care of Worlds: A Psychosystems Approach to Pastoral Care and Counseling.* Nashville: Abingdon Press, 1992.

Greenberg, J. R., and S. A. Mitchell. *Object Relations in Psychoanalytic Theory.* Cambridge: Harvard University Press, 1983.

Greene, J. G. "Psychosocial Influences." In Ruth Formanek, ed. *The Meanings of Menopause: Historical, Medical and Clinical Perspectives.* Hillsdale, N.J.: The Analytic Press, 1990.

Greiner, Donald. *Adultery in the American Novel: Updike, James and Hawthorne.* Columbia: University of South Carolina Press, 1985.

_____. "Body and Soul: John Updike and *The Scarlet Letter*." *Journal of Modern Literature* 15:4 (1989): 475-95.

_____. *John Updike's Novels.* Athens: Ohio University Press, 1984.

_____. "Updike on Hawthorne." *The Nathaniel Hawthorne Review* 13 (1987): 1-4.

Greven, Philip. *Spare the Child: The Religious Roots of Punishment and the Psychological Impact of Physical Abuse.* New York: Vintage, 1990.

Grotstein, James S. "Nothingness, Meaninglessness, Chaos, and the 'Black Hole' III: Self- and Interactional Regulation and the Background Presence of Primary Identification." *Contemporary Psychoanalysis* 27 (1991): 1-33.

Guggenbuhl-Craig, Adolf. *Power in the Helping Professions.* Dallas: Spring, 1971.

Gunn, Giles. *The Interpretation of Otherness: Literature, Religion and the American Imagination.* New York: Oxford University Press, 1979.

_____. "Literary Criticism and Its Relation to Religion." *Religious Studies and Theology* 7 (1987): 7-18.

Gutheil, Thomas G. and Glen Gabbard. "The Concept of Boundaries in Clinical Practice: Theoretical and Risk Management Decisions." *American Journal of Psychiatry* 150 (1993): 188-96.

Harris, Trudier. "Escaping Slavery but Not Its Images." In Henry Louis Gates, Jr., and K. A. Appiah, eds. *Toni Morrison: Critical Perspectives Past and Present.* New York: Amistad, 1993.

Hartmann, Ernest. *Boundaries in the Mind: A New Psychology of Personality.* New York: Basic Books, 1991.

Herman, Judith. *Trauma and Recovery: The Aftermath of Violence—from Domestic Abuse to Political Terror.* New York: Basic Books, 1992.

Heyward, Carter. *Our Passion for Justice: Images of Power, Sexuality and Liberation.* New York: Pilgrim Press, 1984.

_____. *Touching Our Strength: The Erotic as Power and the Love of God.* San Francisco: Harper & Row, 1989.

_____. *When Boundaries Betray Us.* San Francisco: HarperSanFrancisco, 1993.

Hillman, James. *Inter Views: Conversations with Laura Pozzo on Psychotherapy, Biography, Love, Soul, Dreams, Work, Imagination, and the State of the Culture.* San Francisco: Harper Colophon Books, 1983.

Hinkle, John E. and Gregory A. Hinkle. "Surrendering the Self: Pastoral Counseling at the Limits of Culture and Psychotherapy." *The Journal of Pastoral Care* 46 (1992): 103-16.

Holbrook, David and Elizabeth Poston. *The Cambridge Hymnal.* Cambridge: Cambridge University Press, 1967.

Holloway, Karla F. C. *Moorings and Metaphors: Figures of Culture and Gender in Black Woman's Literature.* New Brunswick, N.J.: Rutgers University Press, 1992.

Hunt, George. *John Updike and the Three Great Secret Things: Sex, Religion, and Art.* Grand Rapids: Eerdmans, 1980.

Hunter, Anne Marie. "Numbering the Hairs on Our Heads." *Journal of Feminist Studies in Religion* 8:2 (1992): 7-26.

Irwin, Alexander C. *Eros Toward the World: Paul Tillich and the Theology of the Erotic.* Minneapolis: Fortress Press, 1991.

_____. "The Faces of Desire: Tillich on 'Essential Libido,' Concupiscence and the Transcendence of Estrangement." *Encounter* 51 (1990): 339-58.

Jasper, David, ed. *Postmodernism, Literature and the Future of Theology.* New York: St. Martin's Press, 1993.

Jordan, Judith V. "Empathy and the Mother-Daughter Relationship." In Judith V. Jordan, Alexandra G. Kaplan, Jean Baker Miller, Irene P. Stiver, and Janet L. Surrey, eds. *Women's Growth in Connection: Writings from the Stone Center.* New York: The Guilford Press, 1991.

Jordan, Merle. *Taking on the Gods: The Task of the Pastoral Counselor.* Nashville: Abingdon Press, 1985.

Joy, Morny. "Conclusion: Divine Reservations." In Harold Coward and Toby Foshay, eds. *Derrida and Negative Theology.* Albany: State University of New York Press, 1992.

Joyce, James. *The Dubliners.* New York: Viking Compass, 1968.

Karaban, Roslyn A. "The Sharing of Cultural Variation." *The Journal of Pastoral Care* 45 (1991): 25-34.

Kirkland-Harris, Linda. Personal correspondence, 1994.

Kohut, Heinz. *The Analysis of the Self: A Systematic Approach to the Psychoanalytic Treatment of Narcisstic Personality Disorders.* New York: International Universities Press, 1971.

_____. *The Restoration of the Self.* New York: International Universities Press, 1977.

Kort, Wesley A. " 'Religion and Literature' in Postmodern Contexts." *Journal of the American Academy of Religion* 58:4 (1990): 575-88.

Kundera, Milan. *The Joke.* Translated from Czech by Michael Henry Heim. New York: Penguin, 1982.

_____. *The Unbearable Lightness of Being.* Translated from Czech by Michael Henry Heim. New York: Harper & Row, 1987.

Lawrence, D. H. *Studies in Classic American Literature.* Garden City, N.Y.: Doubleday Anchor Books, 1951.

Lebacqz, Karen. *Professional Ethics: Power and Paradox.* Nashville: Abingdon Press, 1985.

Lebacqz, Karen and Ronald Barton. *Sex in the Parish.* Louisville: John Knox Press, 1991.

Loomer, Bernard. "Two Conceptions of Power." *Process Studies* 6 (Spring 1976): 5-32.

McCarthy, Marie. "Empathy: A Bridge Between." *The Journal of Pastoral Care* 46 (1992): 119-28.

McDargh, John. *Psychoanalytic Object Relations Theory and the Study of Religion: On Faith and the Imaging of God.* New York: University Press of America, 1983.

McFague, Sallie. *Metaphorical Theology: Models of God in Religious Language.* Philadelphia: Fortress Press, 1982.

Meissner, William W. *Life and Faith: Psychological Perspectives on Religious Experience.* Washington, D.C.: Georgetown University Press, 1987.

_____. *Psychoanalysis and Religious Experience.* New Haven, Conn.: Yale University Press, 1984.

_____. "Psychoanalytic Aspects of Religious Experience." *Annual of Psychoanalysis* 6 (1978): 103-41.

_____. "The Psychology of Religious Experience." *Communio* 4 (1977): 3659.

_____. "Religious Thinking as Transitional Conceptualization." *The Psychoanalytic Review* 79 (1992): 175-96.

Miller, Jean Baker. *Toward a New Psychology of Women.* Boston: Beacon Press, 1976.

Mitchell, Stephen A. *Hope and Dread in Psychoanalysis.* New York: Basic Books, 1993.

Moi, Toril. *Sexual/Textual Politics.* London: Routledge, 1985.

Morey, Ann-Janine. *Religion and Sexuality in American Literature.* Cambridge: Cambridge University Press, 1992.

Morey-Gaines, Ann-Janine. "Religion and Sexuality in Walker Percy, William Gass, and John Updike: Metaphors of Embodiment in the Anthrocentric Imagination." *Journal of the American Academy of Religion* 51:4 (1983): 595-609.

Morrison, Toni. *Beloved.* New York: Penguin Books, 1987.

_____. *Playing in the Dark: Whiteness and the Literary Imagination.* Cambridge, Mass.: Harvard University Press, 1992.

_____. *Raceing, Justice, En-gendering Power: Essays on Anita Hill, Clarence Thomas, and the Construction of Social Reality.* New York: Pantheon Books, 1992.

_____. *Sula.* New York: Knopf, 1974.

Moss, John. *Sex and Violence in the Canadian Novel: The Ancestral Present.* Toronto: McClelland and Stewart, 1977.

Murdoch, Iris. *The Fire and the Sun: Why Plato Banished the Artists.* New York: Oxford University Press, 1977.

_____. *The Sovereignty of the Good.* New York: Schocken, 1971.

_____. *Nuns and Soldiers.* New York: Penguin Books, 1981.

_____. *Under the Net.* New York: Penguin Books, 1954.

Nelson, James B. *Body Theology: God's Presence in Man's World.* Louisville: Westminster/John Knox Press, 1992.

Newman, Judie. *John Updike.* New York: St. Martin's Press, 1988.

Orr, Judith. "Ministry with Working Class Women." *The Journal of Pastoral Care* 45 (1991): 343-53.

Patton, John. *Pastoral Care in Context: An Introduction to Pastoral Care.* Louisville: Westminster/John Knox, 1993.

Pellauer, Mary, Barbara Chester, and Jane Boyajian, eds. *Sexual Assault and Abuse: A Handbook for Clergy and Religious Professionals.* San Francisco: Harper & Row, 1987.

Person, Ethel. "Sexuality as the Mainstay of Identity: Psychoanalytic Perspectives." *Signs* 5 (1980): 605-30.

Peterson, Marilyn. *At Personal Risk: Boundary Violations in Professional-Client Relationships.* New York: Norton, 1992.

Piercy, Marge. *The Moon Is Always Female: Poems.* New York: Knopf, 1980.

Poling, James. *The Abuse of Power: A Theological Problem.* Nashville: Abingdon Press, 1991.

Randell, Robert. *Pastor and Parish: The Psychological Care of Ecclesiastic Conflicts.* New York: Human Science Press, 1987.

Randour, M. L., and J. Bondanza. "The Concept of God in the Psychological Formation of Females." *Psychoanalytic Psychology* 4 (1987): 301-313.

Rediger, Lloyd. *Ministry and Sexuality: Cases, Counseling and Care.* Minneapolis: Fortress Press, 1990.

Rice, C. A. and J. S. Rutan. *Inpatient Group Psychotherapy: A Psychodynamic Perspective.* New York: MacMillan Press, 1987.

Rizzuto, A. M. *The Birth of the Living God: A Psychoanalytic Study.* Chicago: The University of Chicago Press, 1979.

Ross, Sinclair. *As for Me and My House.* Toronto: McClelland & Stewart, 1941.

Rothstein, Mervyn. "Morrison Discusses New Novel." *New York Times,* August 29, 1987.

Rubenstein, Roberta. "Pariahs and Community." In Henry Louis Gates, Jr., and K. A. Appiah, eds. *Toni Morrison: Critical Perspectives Past and Present.* New York: Amistad, 1993.

Ruf, Henry. "The Origin of the Debate over Ontotheology and Deconstruction in the Texts of Wittgenstein and Derrida." In Henry Ruf, ed. *Religion, Ontotheology and Deconstruction.* New York: Paragon House, 1989.

Rutter, Peter. *Sex in the Forbidden Zone: When Men in Power—Therapists, Doctors, Clergy, Teachers and Others—Betray Women's Trust.* Los Angeles: Jeremy Tarcher, 1989.

Saiving, Valerie. "The Human Situation: A Feminine View." *The Journal of Religion* 40 (April, 1960): 100-112.

Saltman, V. and R. S. Solomon. "Incest and the Multiple Personality." *Psychological Reports* 50 (1982): 1127-1141.

Sandler, J. "The Background of Safety." *International Journal of Psychoanalysis* 41 (1960): 352-56.

Sandler, J., and B. Rosenblatt. "The Concept of the Representational World." *Psychoanalytic Study of the Child* 17 (1962):128-45.

Sarton, May. "Evening Music." In Serena Sue Hilsinger and Lois Brynes, eds. *Selected Poems of May Sarton.* New York, Norton, 1978.

Scarry, Elaine. *The Body in Pain: The Making and Unmaking of the World.* New York: Oxford University Press, 1985.

Schiff, James A. *Updike's Version: Rewriting the Scarlet Letter.* Columbia: University of Missouri, 1992.

Schlauch, Chris. "Empathy as the Essence of Pastoral Psychotherapy." *The Journal of Pastoral Care* 44 (1990), 3-17.

_____. "Pastoral Psychology." Boston, Mass.: Unpublished paper, 1993.

_____. *Faithful Companioning.* Forthcoming.

Scruton, Roger. *Sexual Desire: A Moral Philosophy of the Erotic.* New York: The Free Press, 1986.

Selden, Raman and Peter Widdowson. "Reader-oriented Theories." In *A Reader's Guide to Contemporary Literary Theory,* third edition. Lexington: The University of Kentucky Press, 1993.

Shengold, Leonard. *"The Boy Will Come to Nothing": Freud's Ego Ideal and Freud as Ego Ideal.* New Haven: Yale University Press, 1993.

Sixty Hymns from Songs of Zion: A Hymnal Supplement. Whittier, California: Praise Publications, 1977.

Smith, Jr., Archie. *The Relational Self: Ethics and Therapy from a Black Church Perspective.* Nashville: Abingdon Press, 1982.

_____. "Black Liberation and Process Theologies." *Process Studies* 16 (1987): 174-90.

Smith, Huston. "The View from Everywhere: Ontotheology and the Post-Nietzschean Deconstruction of Metaphysics." In Henry Ruf, ed. *Religion, Ontotheology and Deconstruction.* New York: Paragon House, 1989.

_____. "Postmodern's Impact on the Study of Religion." *Journal of the American Academy of Religion* 54 (1990): 653-670.

Smith, Joshua. Quoted in David Holbrook and Elizabeth Poston. *The Cambridge Hymnal.* Cambridge: Cambridge University Press, 1967.

Smith, Valerie. " 'Circling the Subject': History and Narrative in *Beloved.*" In Henry Louis Gates, Jr., and K. A. Appiah, ed. *Toni Morrison: Critical Perspectives Past and Present.* New York: Amistad, 1993.

Spero, Moshe Halevi. *Religious Objects as Psychological Structures: A Critical Integration of Object Relations Theory, Psychotherapy and Judaism.* Chicago: The University of Chicago Press, 1992.

Stepto, Robert B. " 'Intimate Things in Place': A Conversation with Toni Morrison." In Henry Louis Gates, Jr., and K. A. Appiah, eds. *Toni Morrison: Critical Perspectives Past and Present.* New York: Amistad, 1993.

Stoller, Robert. J. *Perversion.* New York: Pantheon, 1975.

_____. "Patients' Responses to Their Own Case Reports." *Journal of the American Psychoanalytic Association* 36 (1988): 371-91.

_____. "Eros and Polis: What Is This Thing Called Love?" *Journal of the American Psychoanalytic Association* 39 (1991): 1065-1102.

Taylor, Charles. *The Malaise of Modernity.* Concord, Ontario: Anansi, 1991.

Taylor, Mark C. *Altarity.* Chicago: University of Chicago Press, 1987.

_____. In Harold Coward and Toby Foshay, eds. *Derrida and Negative Theology.* Albany: State University of New York Press, 1992.

Thistlethwaite, Susan. *God, Race and Sex: Christian Feminism in Black and White.* New York: Crossroads, 1991.

Titchener, J. L. "Post-traumatic Decline: A Consequence of Unresolved Destructive Drives." In C. R. Figley, ed. *Trauma and Its Wake, Vol. II.* New York: Brunner/Mazel, 1986.

Tucker, Lindsey. "Introduction." In L. Tucker, ed. *Critical Essays on Iris Murdoch.* New York: G. K. Hall, 1992.

Updike, John. *A Month of Sundays.* New York: Fawcett Press, 1975.

Uphaus, Suzanne Henning. *John Updike.* New York: Frederick Ungar Publishing, 1980.

Vergote, A. *Guilt and Desire: Religious Attitudes and Their Pathological Derivatives.* Translated by M. H. Wood. New Haven, Conn.: Yale University Press, 1988.

Walsh, Thomas G. "Deconstruction, Countersecularization, and Communicative Action: Prelude to Metaphysics." In Henry Ruf, ed. *Religion, Ontotheology and Deconstruction.* New York: Paragon House, 1989.

West, Cornel. "Black Leadership and the Pitfalls of Racial Reasoning." In Toni Morrison, ed. *Raceing, Justice, En-gendering Power: Essays on Anita Hill, Clarence Thomas, and the Construction of Social Reality.* New York: Pantheon Books, 1992.

Wiley, Christine. "A Ministry of Empowerment: A Holistic Model for Pastoral Counseling in the African American Community." *The Journal of Pastoral Care* 45 (1991): 355-64.

Williams, Delores. "Women's Oppression and Lifeline Politics in Black Women's Religious Narratives." *Journal of Feminist Studies in Religion* 1:2 (1985): 59-171.

Williams, James G. *The Bible, Violence and the Sacred: Liberations from the Myth of Sanctioned Violence.* New York: HarperCollins, 1991.

Willis, Susan. "Eruptions of Funk: Historizing Toni Morrison." In Henry Louis Gates, Jr., and K. A. Appiah, eds. *Toni Morrison: Critical Perspectives Past and Present.* New York: Amistad, 1993.

Wilmore, Gayraud S. *Black Religion and Black Radicalism: An Interpretation of the Religious History of Afro-American People.* 2nd. ed., Revised and enlarged. New York: Maryknoll, 1983.

Wilmore, Gayraud S., and James H. Cone. *Black Theology: A Documentary History: 1966-1979.* New York: Orbis Books, 1979.

Wimberly, Edward P. *Pastoral Care in the Black Church.* Nashville, Abingdon Press, 1979.

_____. "The Healing Tradition of the Black Church and Modern Science: A Model of Traditioning." *The Journal of the Interdenominational Theological Center* 11 (1983/1984): 19-30.

_____. *African American Pastoral Care.* Nashville: Abingdon Press, 1991.

Winnicott, D. W. *The Maturational Process and the Facilitating Environment.* New York: International Universities Press, 1960.

SUBJECT INDEX

AUTHOR INDEX